Am

Quick Reference

Que Quick Reference Series

Trudi Reisner

Ami Pro 3 Quick Reference.

Copyright © **1992 by Que® Corporation.**

All rights reserved. Printed in the United States of America.
No part of this book may be used or reproduced in any
form or by any means, or stored in a database or retrieval
system, without prior written permission of the publisher
except in the case of brief quotations embodied in critical
articles and reviews. Making copies of any part of this book
for any purpose other than your own personal use is a
violation of United States copyright laws. For information,
address Que Corporation, 11711 North College Avenue,
Suite 140, Carmel, IN 46032.

Library of Congress Catalog Number: 92-61621

ISBN: 1-56529-113-1

This book is sold *as is*, without warranty of any kind, either
express or implied, respecting the contents of this book,
including but not limited to implied warranties for the
book's quality, performance, merchantability, or fitness for
any particular purpose. Neither Que Corporation nor its
dealers or distributors shall be liable to the purchaser or
any other person or entity with respect to any liability, loss,
or damage caused or alleged to be caused directly or indi-
rectly by this book.

94   93   4   3   2

Interpretation of the printing code: the rightmost
double-digit number is the year of the book's printing; the
rightmost single-digit number is the number of the book's
printing. For example, a printing code of 92-4 shows that
the fourth printing of the book occurred in 1992.

This book is based on Version 3.0 of Ami Pro.

CREDITS

Publisher
Lloyd J. Short

Production Editor
Pamela D. Wampler

Editor
J. Christopher Nelson

Technical Editor
John Khoury

Production Team
Claudia Bell
Paula Carroll
Bob LaRoche
Laurie Lee
Jay Lesandrini
Cindy L. Phipps
Linda Seifert
Johnna VanHoose

TRADEMARK ACKNOWLEDGMENTS

All terms mentioned in this book that are known to be trademarks or service marks have been appropriately capitalized. Que cannot attest to the accuracy of this information. Use of a term in this book should not be regarded as affecting the validity of any trademark or service mark.

Ami Pro is a trademark of SAMNA Corporation.

TABLE OF CONTENTS

AN AMI PRO OVERVIEW

Ami Pro is a powerful and easy-to-use word processing program that enables you to create professional-looking documents as well as format, lay out, and enhance those documents.

Ami Pro 3.0 provides all the excellent word processing features that Ami Pro users have enjoyed in earlier versions of the program. To these features, Ami Pro 3.0 adds many new ones. Some of these new features will save you time performing daily word processing tasks.

The following table summarizes the new features:

New feature	Use
Envelopes	Creates and prints addresses and return addresses on envelopes.
Fonts	Provides 13 scalable Adobe Type Manager fonts.

New feature	Use
Grammar checker	Proofreads documents for correct grammar and language use.
Help	Provides on-line, context-sensitive Help for any function. Help includes an Index and a QuickStart Tutorial that contains beginner's lessons.
Image Processing	Enables you to fine-tune the appearance of gray-scale images.
Importing/Exporting	Provides import/export filters for Word for Windows 2.0, OfficeWriter, and ProWrite.
Labels	Creates and prints address labels on Avery labels.
Lists	Renumbers lists automatically; right-aligns numbers in a list; enables you to insert bullets in a list.
Print	Prints both landscape and portrait pages in one print job (Windows 3.1 only).
Style Sheets	Enables you to preview a style sheet, including a description of the style sheet; provides automated style sheets for creating letters, memos, labels, newsletters, and so on.
Table of Authorities	Enables you to create a table of authorities for legal briefs.

New feature	Use
Table of Contents	Enables you to create up to nine levels in a table of contents.
SmartIcons	Provides shortcuts for choosing commands. You can customize the SmartIcons palette for easy access to often-used commands.

The Ami Pro Screen

When you start Ami Pro, the program appears in an application window. An application window includes a title bar, a menu bar, the SmartIcons palette, and the status bar.

When you open a new or existing Ami Pro document, the document appears in a *document window*. A document window includes a title bar and horizontal and vertical scroll bars.

Title bar

The title bar, located at the top of a window, displays the name of the application—in this case, Ami Pro—and the name of the document.

Menu bar

The menu bar, located below the title bar, contains pull-down menus that list Ami Pro commands.

SmartIcons palette   Title bar   Menu bar

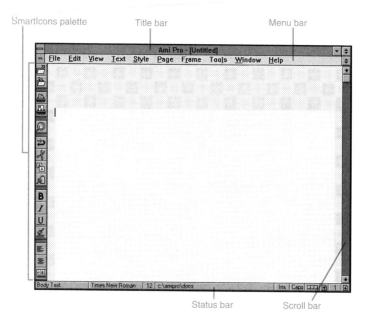

Status bar   Scroll bar

SmartIcons palette

The SmartIcons palette, located directly below the
menu bar, contains buttons for the most frequently
used Ami Pro commands. To perform tasks quickly,
you can click buttons on the SmartIcons palette
rather than choose commands from menus. You
also can move the SmartIcons palette to different
locations on the screen.

Scroll bars

At the right side of each document window is a
vertical scroll bar that contains an up arrow, a down
arrow, and a scroll box. At the bottom of each
document window is a horizontal scroll bar that
contains a left arrow, a right arrow, and a scroll box.

Status bar

The status bar, located at the bottom of the application window, contains information, indicators, and messages. The Style button, Font button, and Font Size button appear at the left end of the status bar. The Path button appears in the center of the status bar. Insert, Typeover, Number Lock, Caps Lock, SmartIcons Hide/Display, Page Number Status, and the Page Arrow button appear at the right end of the status bar.

Using a Mouse

You can use a mouse with Ami Pro. If you do not have a mouse, consider investing in one because a mouse can speed up your work significantly. You can use the SmartIcons, one of the exceptional features of Ami Pro, only if you have a mouse.

The following table describes the basic mouse actions you use in Ami Pro:

Mouse action	Description
Point	Place the mouse pointer on the item to which you want to point.
Click	Point to the item and then press and release the left mouse button one time.
Double-click	Point to the item and then press and release the left mouse button two times in rapid succession.
Drag	Point to the item and then hold down the left mouse button as you slide the mouse across a surface, such as your desk.

Selecting Text

Purpose

Defines a portion of text you want to type over, delete, move, copy, or enhance. Ami Pro highlights text you select.

To select text by using the mouse

Place the mouse pointer at the beginning of the text you want to select, hold down the left mouse button, and drag the mouse pointer across the text.

To select text by using other mouse methods

You also can use the following techniques for selecting text with the mouse:

- To select a word, double-click the word.

- To select multiple words, double-click the first word and drag the mouse pointer across the additional words.

- To select a line of text, hold down the left mouse button and drag the mouse pointer from the beginning to the end of the line of text.

- To select a sentence, hold down Ctrl and click anywhere within the sentence.

- To select multiple sentences, hold down Ctrl, double-click the first sentence, and drag the mouse pointer across the additional sentences.

- To select a paragraph, hold down Ctrl and double-click anywhere within the paragraph.

■ To select multiple paragraphs, hold down
Ctrl, double-click the first paragraph, and
drag the mouse pointer across the additional
paragraphs.

■ To select a block of text, place the mouse
pointer at the beginning of the text you want to
select, click the left mouse button, and then
hold down Shift as you click the end of the
block of text.

To deselect text by using the mouse

Click anywhere in the document outside the
selected text.

To select text by using the keyboard

You can use any of the following keyboard techniques to select text:

■ To select one character to the right of the
insertion point, press Shift+→.

■ To select one character to the left of the
insertion point, press Shift+←.

■ To select the line above the insertion point,
press Shift+↑.

■ To select the line below the insertion point,
press Shift+↓.

■ To select text from the insertion point to the
end of the line, press Shift+End.

■ To select text from the insertion point to the
beginning of the line, press Shift+Home.

■ To select text from the insertion point to the
end of the document, press Shift+Ctrl+End.

■ To select text from the insertion point
to the beginning of the document, press
Shift+Ctrl+Home.

To deselect text by using the keyboard

Press ↑, ↓, ←, →, or Esc; or Shift+↑, Shift+↓,
Shift+ ←, or Shift+→.

Choosing Menu Commands

A *menu* is a list of commands. In Windows programs, the menu names appear in the menu bar at
the top of the screen under the title bar.

You can choose menu commands by using the
mouse or the keyboard. The easiest way to choose
commands is to use the mouse. However, Ami Pro
does provide an easy way to choose menu commands by using the keyboard: *mnemonics*.

Mnemonics are memory aids. In Ami Pro, mnemonics can help you to remember certain keyboard
commands.

To choose a menu command by using the mouse

1. Click the name of the menu that contains the
   command you want to choose.

   Ami Pro displays that menu.

2. You have two ways to choose the command
   with the mouse:

   Click the command you want to choose.

   Drag the mouse pointer down the menu to
   highlight the command you want to choose,
   and then release the mouse button.

   If you choose a command that is followed by
   an ellipsis (...), Ami Pro displays a dialog box;
   otherwise, Ami Pro executes the command.

To choose a menu command by using mnemonics

1. Hold down Alt to activate the menu bar and press the underlined letter in the menu name. To choose the Edit menu, for example, press Alt+E.

2. Press the underlined letter in the command name. To choose Copy, for example, press C.

   If you choose a command that is followed by an ellipsis (...), Ami Pro displays a dialog box; otherwise, Ami Pro executes the command.

Note

Letters that are underlined on-screen appear in boldface blue type in this book. When two keys are separated by a plus sign, you hold down the first key as you press the second key.

Choosing Dialog Box Options

Dialog boxes provide information, messages, options, and warnings, and they enable you to set up certain menu commands.

When you choose a menu command that is followed by an ellipsis (...), Ami Pro displays a dialog box where you supply additional information about that com-mand. Dialog boxes contain various boxes and buttons you use to supply that command information.

To type information in a text box

A *text box* is a rectangular box where you type text or other information.

To type information in a text box, do one of the following:

■ Click inside the text box, and then type the information.

■ Hold down Alt, press the underlined letter in the text box name, and then type the information.

■ Move to the text box by pressing Tab or Shift+Tab, and then type the information.

To choose or turn off a check box

A *check box* is a small square box that appears next to an option. When an option is chosen (turned on), an X appears in its check box. You can choose more than one check box from a set of options.

To choose or turn off an option that has a check box, do one of the following:

■ Click the check box.

■ Hold down Alt, and then press the underlined letter in the option name.

■ Move to the option by pressing Tab or Shift+Tab, and then press the space bar.

To choose or turn off an option button

An *option button* is a small round button that appears next to an option. When an option is chosen (turned on), a black dot appears in its option button. You can choose only one option button from each set of options.

To choose or turn off an option that has an option button, do one of the following:

■ Click the option button.

■ Hold down Alt, and then press the underlined letter in the option name.

■ Move to that set of option buttons by pressing Tab or Shift+Tab, and then press ↑ or ↓ to choose the option you want.

To choose an option from a closed list box

A *closed list box* (a *pull-down list*) is a small rectangular box that contains the name of the currently chosen option and has an arrow at the end of the box.

You can choose an option from a closed list box by doing one of the following:

■ Click the arrow at the end of the list box, drag the mouse pointer down the list to highlight the option, and then release the mouse button.

■ Hold down Alt and press the underlined letter in the list box name. Press ↑ or ↓ to highlight the option, and then press Enter.

■ Move to the list box by pressing Tab or Shift+Tab, and press space bar to display the list. Press ↑ or ↓ to highlight the option, and then press Enter.

To choose an option from an open list box

An *open list box* is a rectangular box that contains a list of options and may have a scroll bar at the side of the box.

You can choose an option from an open list box by doing one of the following:

■ Use the scroll bar to display the option you want to choose, and then click the option.

■ Hold down Alt and press the underlined letter in the list box name. Press ↑ or ↓ to highlight the option, and then press Enter.

■ Move to the list box by pressing Tab or Shift+Tab. Press ↑ or ↓ to highlight the option, and then press Enter.

To choose a command button

A *command button* is an oblong button that executes a command. The most common command buttons are OK, Cancel, and Close.

To choose a command button, do one of the following:

■ Click the command button.

■ Hold down Alt, and then press the underlined letter in the command button name.

To accept or abandon changes in a dialog box using the keyboard

■ To accept your changes and close the dialog box, press Enter.

■ To abandon your changes and close the dialog box, press Esc.

To access Help in a dialog box

A *question mark button* appears in the upper-right corner of all dialog boxes. Ami Pro provides context-sensitive Help for a specific dialog box.

To access Help in a dialog box, click the question mark button. Or press F1 on the keyboard.

To move a dialog box by using the mouse

1. Click the title bar of the dialog box and hold down the mouse button.

2. Drag the dialog box to the new location and release the mouse button.

To move a dialog box by using the keyboard

1. Press Alt+space bar to open the Control menu.

2. Press Enter to choose the Move command.

3. Press ↑, ↓, ←, or → to move the dialog box to the new location, and then press Enter.

Navigating Ami Pro Documents

You can open as many as nine document windows at a time and switch back and forth between documents. You can move around a document window by using the mouse or the keyboard.

To open a new document

You can use either of the following methods to open a new document:

■ Click the File menu, and then click or drag to choose New.

■ Press Alt+F to choose the File menu, and then press N to choose New.

Note

For instructions on opening an existing document, see *Open*.

To switch between documents

1. Click the Window menu, or press Alt+W.

The Window menu opens. The names of all open documents appear in the document list at the bottom of the menu.

2. Choose a new document by using one of the following techniques:

   Click or drag to choose the document.

   Press ↓ to highlight the document, and then press Enter.

   Type the underlined number of the document, and then press Enter.

To move around a document by using the mouse

Using a mouse is often the easiest way to move around an Ami Pro document; simply click a different location on-screen, or use the scroll bars to move to another area of the document.

You can use the mouse and the scroll bars to navigate a document in the following three ways:

■ Click the up, down, left, or right scroll-bar arrow to move up, down, left, or right in the document. If you hold down the mouse button, the document scrolls continuously.

■ Drag the scroll box up or down (in the vertical scroll bar) to move up or down the document. Drag the scroll box left or right (in the horizontal scroll bar) to move left or right in the document.

■ Click the dark gray area above, below, or to the side of a scroll box to move one window length or width in that direction.

To move around a document by using the keyboard

You can move around an Ami Pro document by using the following keys:

Key(s)	Effect
←	Moves the insertion point one character to the left.
→	Moves the insertion point one character to the right.
↑	Moves the insertion point up one line.
↓	Moves the insertion point down one line.
Ctrl+←	Moves the insertion point one word to the left.
Ctrl+→	Moves the insertion point one word to the right.
Home	Moves the insertion point to the beginning of the line.
End	Moves the insertion point to the end of the line.
PgUp	Moves the insertion point up one screen.
PgDn	Moves the insertion point down one screen.
Ctrl+PgUp	Moves the insertion point up one page.
Ctrl+PgDn	Moves the insertion point down one page.
Ctrl+Home	Moves the insertion point to the beginning of the document.
Ctrl+End	Moves the insertion point to the end of the document.

COMMAND REFERENCE

The Command Reference is an alphabetical listing of Ami Pro commands and features. If you want to learn how to set up a numbered list, for example, see *Lists*.

All entries present information in the same format. A brief introductory paragraph summarizes the purpose of the command. Then, step-by-step instructions explain how to use the command. Within *Lists*, for example, you can find information on creating numbered or bulleted lists and on editing lists. Some entries also have cautions, reminders, and notes to help you avoid errors and to show you alternative ways to accomplish the tasks.

As you read this book, keep in mind the following conventions:

■ Keys you press, text you type, and letters that are underlined on-screen (in menu names, commands, and dialog box options) appear in boldface blue type.

■ When you see two keys separated by a plus sign (a *key combination*), you hold down the first key, such as Alt or Shift, as you press the second key.

■ When you see two keys separated by a comma, you press and release the first key, and then press and release the second key.

■ Screen displays and messages appear in a special typeface.

■ This book is extensively cross-referenced. For more information about a command or function, see the entry referenced in *italic* type.

Where applicable, this book also provides alternative methods for accomplishing tasks.

> **REMINDER:** When using the keyboard to choose a menu or a dialog box option, you hold down Alt as you press the underlined letter.

If you are new to the Windows environment, begin by becoming familiar with the Windows features described in "An Ami Pro Overview."

Adding Text

Purpose

Adds text to existing text.

Insert mode (the default mode) inserts new text at the insertion point. Existing text moves forward to make room for the new text.

Typeover mode replaces existing text with the new text.

To insert text

1. Place the insertion point where you want to insert new text.

   The INS indicator appears in the status bar.

2. Type the new text.

   Existing text moves to the right and wraps to the next line.

To type over existing text

1. Place the insertion point where you want to begin typing over existing text.

2. Press Ins (the Insert key) to turn on Typeover mode.

   The TYPE indicator appears in the status bar.

3. Type the new text over the old text.

4. Press Ins again to return to Insert mode.

Alignment

Purpose

Aligns text relative to the left and right margins and the center of the page.

To align text

1. Select the text you want to align. (You can select the entire document.)

2. Choose Text Alignment.

   The Alignment menu appears.

3. Choose one of the following Alignment options:

Option	Effect
Left	Aligns text flush with the left margin (default).
Center	Centers text between the left and right margins.
Right	Aligns text flush with the right margin.
Justify	Spreads text between the left and right margins by expanding or contracting the space between words.

Notes

You also can align text by clicking the Alignment SmartIcons.

See also *SmartIcons*.

Bookmarks

Purpose

Marks selected text in a document with an invisible bookmark. Enables you to return quickly to the bookmark location.

To insert a bookmark

1. Move the insertion point to the location you want to mark, or select the text you want to mark.

2. Choose Edit Bookmarks.

   The Bookmarks dialog box appears.

3. Type the name of the bookmark in the Bookmark text box. A bookmark name can have 1 to 20 characters; can contain letters, numbers, and the underscore (_) character, but not spaces; and must begin with a letter.

4. Choose Add or press Enter to insert the bookmark.

To find a bookmark

1. Choose Edit Bookmarks.

   The Bookmarks dialog box appears.

2. Choose the bookmark name from the Current bookmark list box.

3. Choose Go To or press Enter to find the bookmark.

Bullets

Purpose

Adds bullets, such as dots or diamond symbols, anywhere within your text.

To add bullets

1. Move the insertion point to the location where you want to place a bullet.

2. Choose Edit Insert Bullet.

   The Insert Bullet dialog box appears.

3. Choose a bullet symbol from the Bullet list box.

4. Click OK or press Enter to add the bullets.

Note

See also *Lists* and *Styles*.

Clipboard

Purpose

Stores data temporarily so that you can pass the data from document to document or from application to application. The Clipboard is a feature that all Windows applications can use.

Clipboard commands

The following Ami Pro commands use the Clipboard:

Command	Effect
Edit Cut (Shift+Del)	Cuts selected text or graphics from a document. The data is removed from the document and stored on the Clipboard.
Edit Copy (Ctrl+Ins)	Copies selected text or graphics from a document. The data remains in the document, and a copy is stored on the Clipboard.
Edit Paste (Shift+Ins)	Pastes a copy of the Clipboard's contents into a document at the insertion point.

Notes

You can execute the Clipboard commands by choosing them from the Edit menu; by using the keyboard shortcuts; or by clicking the Cut, Copy, and Paste SmartIcons.

See also *Copy*, *Cut*, *Paste*, and *SmartIcons*.

 Close

Purpose

Closes documents, dialog boxes, and windows.

To close a document

Choose File Close.

Ami Pro closes the document and clears the screen. If you close a document without saving it, a dialog box asks whether you want to save any changes you made.

To close a dialog box

You can use any of the following methods to close a dialog box:

- Double-click the Control menu box (which resembles a file drawer handle) at the left end of the dialog box's title bar.

- Press Alt+space bar to open the Control menu for the dialog box, and then choose Close.

- Press Alt+F4.

- Click OK to save any changes you made and close the dialog box.

- Click Cancel or press Esc to abandon any changes you made and close the dialog box.

- Choose the Close button to close a dialog box that does not contain a Cancel button. When you choose Close, however, some dialog boxes save any changes you made.

To close a window

You can use either of the following methods to close a window:

- Double-click the Control menu box (which resembles a file drawer handle) at the left end of the window's title bar.

- Press Alt+space bar to open the Control menu, and then choose Close.

Columns

Purpose

Creates multiple text columns in which the text begins at the top of a column, continues to the bottom of that column, and then continues from the top of the next column.

To create multiple columns

1. Choose Page Modify Page Layout.

   The Modify Page Layout dialog box appears.

2. From the Modify options, choose the Margins & Columns option.

3. Choose a number from the Number of Columns options.

4. Specify a number, in inches, in the Gutter Width box to modify the space between columns.

5. Choose the Column Balance check box to align the lengths of the columns across the page.

6. Click OK or press Enter to create the columns.

Note

See also *Tables* and *Page Layout.*

Comparing Documents

Purpose

Compares two versions of a document.

> **CAUTION:** Save a backup copy of the original document with a distinctive file name before you begin making comparisons. You can return the original file if you decide not to keep the changes.

To compare two versions of a document

1. Open the original version of the document you want to compare.

2. Choose Tools Doc Compare.

   The Doc Compare dialog box appears.

3. In the File Name text box, type the name of the version (of the document) you want to compare to the original document.

4. Click OK or press Enter.

   The edited document appears on-screen. Revision marks indicate added, replaced, deleted, and moved text.

Notes

To remove all revision marks and restore the current document to its original state when you last saved it, choose File Revert to Saved.

See *Revision Marks*.

Convert File

Purpose

Converts files to and from other formats so that you can exchange files with other programs.

To convert a file from another format

1. Choose File Open.

2. From the List Files of the Type list box, choose the file type you want to convert.

3. From the Directories list box, choose the directory that contains the file you want to convert. A list of the files in the directory appears.

4. Choose the file you want to convert.

5. Click OK or press Enter to begin the conversion process.

To convert a file to another format

See *Save/Save As*.

Available file formats

You can convert files to and from the following formats:

Format	Program Version
Advance Write	
Ami Pro	1.0, 2.0
ASCII	
dBASE III, III PLUS, IV	

Format	Program Version
DCA/FFT	
DCA/RFT	
DIF	
DisplayWrite	4.0, 5.0
E-mail	
Enable	1.5 to 2.5, Lotus 1-2-3 Format
Exec MemoMaker	
Lotus 1-2-3 (DOS)	Release 1.0, 1.0A, 2.0, 2.01, 3.0, 3.1
Lotus Manuscript	Release 2.0, 2.1
Lotus Symphony	Release 1.0, 1.01, 1.1
Microsoft Excel	2.0, 3.0
Microsoft Word (DOS)	4.0, 5.0, 5.1, 5.5
Microsoft Word for Windows	1.0, 2.0
MultiMate	3.3
MultiMate Advantage II	
Multiplan	3.0, 4.2
Navy DIF	
OfficeWriter	
Paradox	Releases up to 3.5
PeachText	Releases up to 2.11
ProWrite	
Rich Text Format (RTF)	
Samna Word	
SmartWare	1.0

Format	Program Version
SuperCalc	3.0, 4.0
Windows Write	
WordPerfect	4.1, 4.2, 5.0, 5.1
WordStar	3.3, 3.4, 4.1. 5.0
WordStar 2000	1.0, 3.0
Works (DOS)	2.0 word processor documents
Works for Windows	Word processor documents

Notes

Earlier versions of Ami Pro file formats are fully compatible with Ami Pro 3.0.

When you have multiple files you want to convert in a single directory, use the CONVERT.SMM macro.

Copy

Purpose

Copies selected text to the Clipboard without removing it from the document. You can paste a copy of the Clipboard's contents to another location in the same document, to a different document, or to a document in another Windows program.

To copy text to the Clipboard

1. Select the text you want to copy to the Clipboard.

2. Choose Edit Copy or press Ctrl+Ins to copy the text to the Clipboard without removing it from the document.

To paste data from the Clipboard to a document

1. Place the insertion point where you want to paste the Clipboard data.

2. Choose Edit Paste or press Shift+Ins to paste a copy of the text.

To copy text without placing it on the Clipboard

1. Select the text you want to copy.

2. Place the insertion point in the new location.

3. Hold down Ctrl+Shift and click the right mouse button.

4. Release the mouse button and Ctrl+Shift to copy the text.

Notes

You can paste the Clipboard's contents into a document any number of times until you cut or copy new text. The new text then replaces the preceding contents of the Clipboard.

You also can copy and paste by clicking the Copy and Paste SmartIcons.

See also *Clipboard*, *Cut*, *Paste*, and *SmartIcons*.

Cut

Purpose

Cuts text from a document and stores it on the
Clipboard. You can paste cut text to another
location in the same document, to a different
document, or to a document in another Windows
program.

To cut text

1. Select the text you want to cut.

2. Choose Edit Cut or press Shift+Del to cut the
   text from the document and store it on the
   Clipboard.

To paste data from the Clipboard to a document

1. Place the insertion point where you want to
   paste the Clipboard data.

2. Choose Edit Paste or press Shift+Ins to paste a
   copy of the text.

To move text without storing it on the Clipboard

1. Select the text you want to move.

2. Place the insertion point in the new location.

3. Hold down Ctrl and click the right mouse
   button.

4. Release the mouse button and Ctrl to move
   the text to the new location.

Notes

You can paste the Clipboard's contents into a
document any number of times until you cut or copy
new text. The new text then replaces the preceding
contents of the Clipboard.

You also can cut and paste by clicking the Cut and
Paste SmartIcons.

See also *Clipboard*, *Copy*, *Paste*, and *SmartIcons*.

Date and Time

Purpose

Inserts the date or time into a document automatically.

> **REMINDER:** Because Ami Pro uses the
> computer's clock to insert the current date
> and time, you must set the computer's clock
> to the correct date and time.

To insert the date or time

1. Place the insertion point where you want the
   date or time to appear in the document.

2. Choose Edit Insert Date/Time.

   The Insert Date/Time dialog box appears.

3. From the Insert options, choose the date and
   time option formats you want Ami Pro to use.

4. From the Style options, choose the date and
   time formats you want Ami Pro to use.

5. Click OK or press Enter.

   Ami Pro automatically inserts the date and time into the document.

Deleting

Purpose

Deletes unwanted text.

> **REMINDERS:** Before you make major changes to a document, use File Save As to save a copy of the document with a different name.
>
> Del and Backspace are repeating keys. If you hold down Del or Backspace, rather than pressing and releasing the key, Ami Pro deletes multiple characters, and the text to the right of the deleted characters moves to the left.

To delete a character

You can delete a character in either of the following ways:

■ Place the insertion point to the left of the character you want to delete, and then press Del.

■ Place the insertion point to the right of the character you want to delete, and then press Backspace.

To delete a word

Use one of the following methods to delete a word:

- Double-click the word you want to delete, and then press Del.

- Place the insertion point to the right of the word you want to delete, and then press Ctrl+Backspace.

- Place the insertion point to the left of the word you want to delete, and then press Ctrl+Del.

To delete a line or lines

1. Drag the mouse pointer down the left margin to select the lines of text or blank lines.

2. Press Del.

To delete a sentence

1. Place the mouse pointer anywhere in the sentence you want to delete.

2. Hold down Ctrl and click the left mouse button to select the sentence.

3. Press Del.

To delete a paragraph

1. Place the mouse pointer in the left margin next to the paragraph you want to delete.

2. Hold down Ctrl and double-click the left mouse button to select the paragraph.

3. Press Del.

To delete a block of text

Select the text you want to delete, and then press
Del.

To delete all text in a document

1. Position the insertion point at the beginning of
   the document.

2. Press Shift+Ctrl+End.

3. Press Del.

Notes

To undo the last deletion, select Edit Undo, press
Ctrl+Z, or click the Undo SmartIcon.

See also *Undo*.

Doc Info

Purpose

Summarizes key information about a document.

To display or edit document summary information

1. Open the document for which you want to
   display or edit document information.

2. Choose File Doc Info.

   The Doc Info dialog box appears.

3. Type the information into the following text
   boxes in the Doc Info dialog box.

Text box	Information
Description	A description of the document. This information appears in the Document Description box in the Save As dialog box when you save the document with a new name.
Keywords	Words for which you may want to search (words that set this document apart from other documents).

4. Click OK or press Enter to save the information.

To view document statistics

1. Open the file for which you want to view document statistics.

2. Choose File Doc Info.

   The Doc Info dialog box appears.

3. View the information about the document.

4. If you have made changes to the document since you last saved it, click the Update button to update the statistics.

5. Click OK or press Enter to save the statistics.

Notes

A summary consists of a brief description of the document and keywords for which to search. Each piece of information can have up to 119 characters. You can sort your files according to any of the information in the document summary.

The document summary also includes document statistics, such as the number of times you save a document; the number of pages, words, and characters in the document; total editing time; and the style sheet on which the document is based.

Envelopes

Purpose

Prints addresses on envelopes.

To print an address on an envelope

1. In a document, select the address you want to print on an envelope.

2. Choose File Print Envelope.

   The Print Envelope dialog box appears.

3. To include a return address, click the Print Return Address check box and type the address in the Return Address box.

4. Specify envelope size by using one of the following options:

   From the Envelope Size options, choose the size of the envelope.

   To specify a different envelope size, click the down arrow next to the More Envelope Sizes list box. A pull-down list of envelope sizes appears. Choose a size from the list.

   To specify a custom envelope size, type the height and width of the envelope in the More Envelope Sizes text boxes, or click the up or down arrow to change the height and width.

5. Click OK or press Enter to print the envelope.

Notes

You also can print an envelope by selecting the Print Envelope SmartIcon.

See also *Labels*.

Equation Editor

Purpose

Enables you to create and edit scientific and mathematical equations directly in your document. The Equation Editor also enables you to save your equations in TEX format for use in other documents or in other applications that support TEX. The Equation Editor also enables you to import TEX files.

To create an equation

1. Place the insertion point where you want to enter the equation.

2. Choose Tools Equations.

   Ami Pro creates a frame at the insertion point, and the Equation icons appear. Also, Equation appears on the menu bar.

3. Type the equation in the Equation frame. You can click special symbol, character, and template icons on the Equation icon bar to include those symbols or templates in the equation. You also can include symbols or templates by selecting Equation from the menu bar.

4. Press Esc twice to exit Equation mode.

To edit an equation

1. Double-click the Equation frame for the equation you want to edit, or select the frame and press Enter.

2. Use any of the following commands to edit the equation:

Command	Effect
Cut or Copy	Removes or copies the selected text or graphics characters and stores them on the Clipboard.
Paste	Pastes the Clipboard's contents into the Equation screen at the insertion point.
View	Magnifies or reduces the size of the equation on-screen.
Limits & Size	Displays the equation, using the operator size specified in the Preferences dialog box. The default limit position for fractions and operators is At Right for Limits & Size Small. The default limit position is Above/Below for Limits & Size Big.
Text Mode	Applies font and character formats to the equation.

Exit

Purpose

Exits Ami Pro and returns to Windows.

To exit Ami Pro and return to Windows

1. Choose File Exit or press Alt+F4.

   If you have not saved your work, a dialog box asks whether you want to save your changes.

2. Choose one of the following options:

Option	Effect
Yes	Saves the document and exits the program.
No	Abandons any changes and exits the program.
Cancel	Cancels the command and remains in the Ami Pro program.

Fast Format

Purpose

Formats text throughout a document quickly. To use the Fast Format command, you must have a mouse.

To format text using Fast Format

1. Select the text that contains the attributes you want to apply.

If you want, add more text attributes.

2. Choose Text Fast Format or press Ctrl+T.

   The mouse pointer changes to an arrow with a paintbrush.

3. Select any text to which you want to apply the same formatting.

   Repeat step 3 as many times as necessary.

4. To disable fast formatting, choose Text Fast Format or press Ctrl+T.

File Manager

Purpose

Lists specified files; changes directories and file attributes. This command also enables you to select, copy, move, rename, or delete several files at one time.

> **REMINDER:** Before you perform any file man-agement operations, be sure you use the File Change directory command and the View com-mands in the File Manager File/Directory list box to list and select the files with which you want to work. Otherwise, you may copy or delete the wrong files.

To list files

1. Choose File File Management.

The Ami Pro File Manager window appears. The files on the current drive and directory appear in the File/Directory list box. Several file-management menu commands appear at the top of the dialog box.

2. Choose View.

3. Choose from the following View options:

Option	Function
*.S?M Files	Lists all Ami Pro documents and macros as well as any other files with a three-character extension beginning with S and ending with M in the current directory.
All	Lists all files in the current directory.
Partial	Enables you to use the asterisk (*) and question mark (?) wildcard characters to list a group of files. To list all files in the current directory, for example, type *.* in the Partial text box in the Partial dialog box. Then click OK or press Enter to close the Partial dialog box.

4. To list files in a different drive or directory, choose File Change Directory. In the Change Directory dialog box, type the path in the Change To text box. Then click OK or press Enter.

The files that match the search criteria appear in the File/Directory list box.

To choose a file or files by using the mouse

1. Click each file name you want to choose.

   Clicking a chosen file in the list deselects it.

2. You now can choose File Copy, File Move, File Rename, or File Delete to execute that command for the chosen files.

To choose a file or files by using the keyboard

1. In the File/Directory list box, press ↑ or ↓ to move the border to the file you want to choose.

2. Press the space bar to highlight the file.

3. Continue pressing ↑ or ↓ and the space bar to choose each file.

   To deselect a file, move the border to the file you want to deselect and press the space bar.

4. You now can choose File Copy, File Move, File Rename, or File Delete to execute that command for the chosen files.

To copy files to another location

1. List and choose the files you want to copy.

2. Choose File Copy.

   The Copy dialog box appears.

3. Type the destination path in the To text box.

4. Click OK or press Enter to copy the file to a new location.

   When you copy a file that has associated graphics and style sheet files, Ami Pro displays the File Copy Options dialog box. Choose from the following Copy options:

Option	Function
Take Associated Graphics Files	Copies associated graphics files and the specified file to the new location.
Take Associated Style Sheet	Copies associated style sheet files and the specified file to the new location. Useful for working with Ami Pro documents on another computer that uses Ami Pro but does not have the same style sheet already available.
Maintain Format	Copies document with embedded formatting. Useful for importing Ami Pro documents into another program that cannot use Ami Pro style sheets, or for working with Ami Pro documents on another computer that does not allow the same Ami Pro style sheets.

To move files to another location

1. List and choose the files you want to move.

2. Choose File Move.

   The Move dialog box appears.

3. Type the destination path in the To text box.

4. Click OK or press Enter to move the file to a new location.

   When you move a file that has associated graphics and style sheet files, Ami Pro displays the File Move Options dialog box. Choose from the following Move options:

Option	Function
Take Associated Graphics Files	Moves associated graphics files and the specified file to the new location.
Take Associated Style Sheet	Moves associated style sheet files and the specified file to the new location. Useful for working with Ami Pro documents on another computer that uses Ami Pro but does not have the same style sheet available.
Maintain Format	Moves document with embedded formatting to the new location. Useful for importing Ami Pro documents into another program that cannot use Ami Pro style sheets, or for working with Ami Pro documents on another computer that does not use the same Ami Pro style sheets.

To rename files

1. List and choose the file(s) you want to rename.
2. Choose File Rename.

   The Rename dialog box appears.
3. Type the new name in the To text box.
4. Click OK or press Enter to rename the file.

To delete files

1. List and choose the file(s) you want to delete.

2. Choose File Delete.

   The Delete dialog box appears.

3. Click OK or press Enter to delete the file.

Notes

An Ami Pro file can have either of two attributes: *read-only* or *read-write*. Read-only means that you can only display the file and cannot edit the file. Read-write means that you can display and edit the file. To change a file's attributes, choose the file you want to change, choose File Attributes, and choose Read Only or Read-Write. Then click OK or press Enter.

See also *Doc Info, Graphics*, and *Styles*.

Find and Replace

Purpose

Finds and replaces specific text, text attributes, or paragraph styles in a document.

To find text or text attributes

1. Place the insertion point where you want to begin the search.

2. Choose Edit Find & Replace or press Ctrl+F.

   The Find & Replace dialog box appears.

3. To search for text, type in the Find text box the
   text you want to find. Choose the Options
   button, and then choose from the following
   Find options:

Option	Function
Whole Word Only	Searches for entire words only; does not find occurrences of the text that are part of other words.
Exact Case	Searches for text with the specified combination of uppercase and lowercase letters.
Exact Attributes	Searches for text with the specified attributes, such as bold, underline, italics, and so on.
Range & Direction	Specifies the area and direction of the search. Choose Beginning of Document to search the entire document or Include Other Text Streams to search other areas in the document. Choose Find Backwards to search backward.

   To search for text attributes, choose the
   Attributes button, and then choose the text
   attributes you want to find.

4. Choose OK to return to the Find & Replace
   dialog box.

5. Click the Find button or press Enter.

The search begins, stopping at the first occurrence of the text or text attribute for which
you are searching. The Find & Replace dialog
box remains open.

6. To search for other occurrences of the text or
   text attributes, click the Find Next button or
   press Enter. To stop the search, choose
   Cancel.

7. Close the Find & Replace dialog box.

To replace text or text attributes

1. Place the insertion point where you want to
   begin the search and replace procedure.

2. Choose Edit Find & Replace or press Ctrl+F.

   The Find & Replace dialog box appears.

3. Use the following methods to indicate the text
   or text attributes you want to replace:

   To replace text, type the text you want to
   replace in the Find text box.

   To replace text attributes, choose the Attributes button, choose the text attributes you
   want to find, and then choose OK to return to
   the Find & Replace dialog box.

   To specify Search options, choose the Options
   button, and then choose the Find options you
   want. Choose OK or press Enter to return to
   the Find and Replace dialog box.

4. If you are replacing text, type the replacement
   text in the Replace With text box. Choose the
   Options button, and then choose from the
   following Replace options:

Option	Function
Exact Case	Searches for text with the specified combination of uppercase and lowercase letters.
Exact Attributes	Searches for text with the specified attributes, such as bold, underline, and italics.

If you are replacing text attributes, choose the Attributes button, and then choose the replacement text attribute.

5. Choose OK to return to the Find & Replace dialog box.

6. Choose the Find button.

   The search begins, stopping at the first occurrence of the text or text attribute for which you are searching. The Find & Replace dialog box remains open.

7. To replace one occurrence of the text or text attribute and then find the next occurrence, choose the Replace & Find Next button. To replace all occurrences of the text or text attribute, choose the Replace Remaining button. To stop the search and replace process, choose Cancel.

   When Ami Pro completes the replace operation, a message displays in the status bar indicating the number of occurrences of the text or text attribute and the number of replacements made.

8. Close the Find & Replace dialog box.

Notes

To find or replace paragraph styles, choose the
Options button, and then choose the Style option
from the Find & Replace Type options in the Find &
Replace Options dialog box. Then choose OK to
return to the Find & Replace dialog box. In the Find
or Replace With text box, type the name of the style
or press the appropriate function key for the style
you want to find or replace.

To find or replace tabs, press Ctrl+Tab in the Find
or Replace With text box. To find or replace carriage
returns, press Ctrl+Enter in the Find or Replace
With text box.

To find or replace special characters, type the
special character enclosed in angle brackets (< >).
To search for a question mark, for example, type
<?> in the Find text box.

To clear paragraph style attributes, choose the
check boxes in the Find & Replace Attributes dialog
box for the attributes you want to clear.

To delete all occurrences of the specified text, type
the text you want to replace in the Find text box and
leave the Replace With text box empty. Then choose
the Replace Remaining button.

Fonts

Purpose

A *font* is a distinctive, named design of a set of
characters, such as Helvetica or Arial. You can
choose fonts and font size independently of style
(such as bold or italic). You can choose any font
that is currently installed in Windows and Ami Pro.
These fonts appear in the Font dialog box.

Ami Pro provides 13 Adobe Type Manager scalable
fonts.

You also can change the color of the fonts. Experiment with the fonts to find one you prefer.

To change the fonts

1. Select the text you want to change.

2. Choose Text Font.

   The Font dialog box appears.

3. From the Face list box, choose the font you want.

   The Sample box displays the effect of the font you choose.

4. From the Size list box, choose the size you want.

5. From the Color bar, choose the color for the font.

6. Click OK or press Enter to change the fonts for the selected text.

Notes

The fonts available in the Face list box depend on what printer driver you are using, the capabilities of your printer, and whether you installed a print cartridge or a soft font package, such as Facelift or MoreFonts.

See also *Style* and *Text Attributes*.

Footnotes

Purpose

Adds footnotes to a document to refer the reader to a source of information or to provide additional data.

Footnotes can appear at the bottom of the page, at the end of the text on a page, or at the end of the document. You can mark footnotes with numbers or a symbol, such as an asterisk.

To create a footnote

1. Place the insertion point in the text where you want the footnote number to appear.

2. Choose Tools Footnotes.

   The Footnotes dialog box appears.

3. Choose the Insert Footnote option.

4. To specify Footnote options, choose the Options button.

   The Footnote Options dialog box appears.

5. Choose from the following Footnote options:

Option	Effect
Make Endnotes	Prints footnotes at the end of the document.
Reset Number On Each Page	Resets the numbering of footnotes on each page instead of consecutively numbering footnotes throughout the document.
Starting Number	Specifies a particular number for the first footnote; 1 is the default.
Margins	Extends the separator line from the left to right margin.
Custom	Specifies the length of the separator line. You can choose the Indent From Left option with this option.

Option	Effect
Indent From Left	Specifies where the separator line starts from the left margin.

6. Click OK or press Enter.

    The Footnote area appears at the bottom of the document window. Ami Pro inserts the footnote reference mark.

7. Type the text of the footnote in the Footnote area.

8. To close the Footnote area and return to the document, press Esc.

To change the footnote number style

1. Place the insertion point in the footnote for which you want to change the footnote number style.

2. Choose Style Modify Style.

    The Modify Style dialog box appears.

3. From the Modify options, choose the Bullets & Numbers option.

4. You can use any of the following alternatives for changing a footnote number style:

    To specify a number style, choose the Number check box, and then choose a number style from the Number Style list box.

    To specify a bullet style, choose the Bullet check box and then choose a bullet style from the Bullet list box.

    To remove the superscript (default footnote reference style) from the footnote number, choose the Superscript check box.

To specify the text attributes you want to apply to the footnote number, choose from Bold, Italic, Underline, Word Underline, and All Caps.

5. Click OK or press Enter to change the footnote number style.

To delete a footnote

1. Place the insertion point on the footnote number of the footnote you want to delete.

2. Select the footnote number in the text.

3. Press Del.

   The message, There is a footnote in the selection to be deleted. Would you like to continue?, appears.

4. Choose Yes or press Enter to remove the footnote number and text.

Note

To view the footnote text on-screen, choose Edit Go To. In the Go To dialog box, choose the Next Item option. Choose Footnote Mark in the Next Item list box, and then choose the Go To ^H button.

Formulas

Purpose

Enables you to create simple mathematical formulas to calculate the contents of cells in a table. You also can add a column or row of numbers in a table using the Quick Add feature.

To create a mathematical formula in a table

1. Place the insertion point in the cell where you want to create a formula—for example, the cell C1.

2. Choose Table Edit Formula.

3. In the Formula text box, type the numbers and mathematical operators you want to include in the formula. To add the number in cell A1 to the number in cell B1, for example, type A1+B1.

4. Click OK or press Enter to create the formula.

   The result of the formula appears in the cell.

To add a column or row using Quick Add

1. Place the insertion point in a cell within the table where you want the row or column total.

2. Choose Table Quick Add.

3. Choose Row or Column.

   The result appears in the cell.

Note

See also *Equations* and *Tables*.

Frames

Purpose

Draws lines and boxes around a block of text, a table, a graphic, or a chart. You also can use a frame to change the position of the text on the page.

To create a frame

1. Choose View Layout Mode to switch to Layout Mode view.

2. Choose Frame Create Frame.

   The Create Frame dialog box appears.

3. In the Size area, specify the width and height for the frame in the Width box and the Height box.

4. In the Position area, specify the placement of the frame's upper-left corner on the page. Enter the number of inches in the Down From Top box and the In From Left box.

5. Click OK or press Enter to insert the frame in the document.

   The frame appears around the selected text.

To remove a frame

1. Select the frame you want to remove.

2. Press Del to remove the frame and its contents.

To modify the lines in the frame

1. Select the frame for which you want to modify the lines.

2. Choose Frame Modify Frame Layout.

   The Modify Frame Layout dialog box appears.

3. From the Frame options, choose Lines & Shadows.

4. From the Lines options, choose All to draw border lines on all sides; choose Left, Right, Top, and Bottom to draw a line on any side.

5. From the Style options, choose a line style.

6. From the Shadow options, choose a shadow style for the frame.

7. Click OK or press Enter to add the lines.

To place text in a frame

1. Double-click the frame to place the insertion point inside the frame. Or select the frame and press Enter.

2. Type the text in the frame. You also can paste text into the frame from the Clipboard.

3. To exit the frame, click outside the frame border or press Esc twice.

To create a drawing frame

1. Select the frame.

2. Choose Tools Drawing.

To create a chart or graph

1. Select the frame.

2. Choose Tools Charting.

Notes

To insert a frame using the mouse, you choose Frame Create Frame; choose the Manual button in the Create Frame dialog box; then click OK. Place the mouse pointer (small picture frame icon) in the upper-left corner where you want the frame to appear. Click the mouse button and drag to the lower-right corner where you want the frame to appear.

You also can create a frame around text and graphics.

See also *Graphics*.

Glossary

Purpose

Inserts text from the glossary into a document when you type or choose the name of the glossary entry.

To create a glossary entry

1. Select the text you want to store as a glossary entry.

   The amount of information you can store depends on the amount of available memory.

2. Choose Edit Mark Text Glossary.

   The Mark Glossary Record dialog box appears.

3. Type a name for the glossary entry in the Record Name text box and click OK.

   The Glossary Data File dialog box appears.

4. Type a name for the glossary data file. You can type a new name or the name of an existing glossary data file.

5. Click OK or press Enter to store the data as a glossary entry and return to the document.

To insert a glossary entry with the menus

1. Place the insertion point where you want to insert the glossary entry.

2. Choose Edit Insert Glossary Record.

The Insert Glossary Record dialog box
appears.

3. From the Glossary Items list box, choose the
   name of the glossary record you want to
   insert.

4. Click the Insert button to insert the glossary
   entry.

To insert a glossary entry with the keyboard

1. Place the insertion point where you want to
   insert the glossary entry.

2. Type the name of the glossary entry.

3. Press Ctrl+K to insert the glossary entry.

Notes

To store text, styles, and page layout information
and recall that information to create, edit, or format
a document, you can use Style Sheets.

See also *Styles.*

Grammar

Purpose

Proofreads documents for correct grammar, style,
punctuation, and use of language.

Tip

You can use the grammar checker as a proofreading
check before you print the document. Grammar
checking a document does not eliminate the need
for proofreading, but does reduce the amount of
proofreading you need to do.

To check grammar in a document

1. Choose Tools Grammar Check.

   The Grammar Checker dialog box appears.

2. If desired, click the down arrow next to the Use Grammar and Style Set list box to see a pull-down list of Grammar and Style options. Then choose an option from the list.

3. If desired, choose from the following Preferences options to customize the Grammar Check command:

Option	Function
Show Readability Statistics	Displays the Readability Statistics box. The Readability Statistics box shows the number of characters, words, sentences, and paragraphs in the text and several standard measurements of the document's readability.
Show Explanations	Displays an explanation of the highlighted rule in the Grammar Checker dialog box.
Check From Beginning of Document	Searches through the entire main document text stream, regardless of the location of the insertion point. Deselect this option if you want the search to start from the current position of the insertion point.

Option	Function
Include Other Text Streams	Searches the main document text and all other lower-priority streams in the grammar check.
Check In Draft Mode	Searches a fixed frame, footnote, or header, instead of the main text of the document.

4. If desired, choose Options in order to choose additional Grammar Check options.

   The Grammar Check Options dialog box appears.

5. Choose from the following Grammar Check options:

Option	Function
Grammar Rules	Specifies the basic grammar rules, usage, and punctuation the Grammar Checker should use to check the grammar in the document.
Style Rules	Specifies a particular writing style to check the effectiveness of sentences and word choice.
Word Order Rules	Checks for sentences that contain split infinitives, consecutive nouns, and prepositional phrases.

6. Click OK or press Enter to close the Grammar Checker Options dialog box.

7. To start the grammar check, click OK or press Enter in the Grammar Checker dialog box.

8. If the Grammar Checker finds an error in grammar or style, choose one of the following options to correct the error or to continue checking grammar:

Option	Function
Skip	Skips the current suggestion and does not change the sentence.
Skip Rule	Skips the rule that appears in the Sugges-tions box (and similar rules within a group of grammar or style rules) for the rest of the document.
Next Sentence	Skips the current suggestion, skips the rest of the errors in this sentence, and checks the following sentence.
Replace	Executes the sugges-tion and changes the sentence. If you want to change the sentence but not in the way suggested, press Alt+F6 or click the document to activate the document. Then make the changes to the sentence in the document and choose the Resume button to continue checking grammar.

Option	Function
Cancel	Exits the Grammar Checker.

When Ami Pro reaches the end of the document, the Readability Statistics box appears,
showing the number of characters, words,
sentences, and paragraphs in the text and
several standard measurements of the
document's readability.

9. Choose Close when you finish reading the
   statistics.

   Ami Pro returns to the document.

Notes

You can choose Grammar Check from the Tools
menu; however, adding the Grammar Check
SmartIcon to the SmartIcons palette enables you
to choose the command much more quickly.

See also *Spelling* and *Thesaurus*.

Graphics

Purpose

Adds graphics to a document.

Ami Pro's powerful AmiDraw feature enables you to
mix text, type, and pictures and to edit and enhance
the graphics you create. This feature also enables
you to use graphics from a variety of sources.

To create a graphics frame

1. Choose View Layout Mode to switch to Layout Mode view.

2. Choose Frame Create Frame.

   The Create Frame dialog box appears.

3. In the Size area, specify the width and height for the frame in the Width box and the Height box.

4. In the Position area, specify the placement of the frame's upper-left corner on the page. Enter the number of inches in the Down From Top box and the In From Left box.

5. Click OK or press Enter to insert the frame in the document.

   The frame appears in the document. You now can type text in or import a graphic into the frame.

To import a graphic

1. Choose View Layout Mode to switch to Layout Mode view.

2. Place the insertion point at the top of the frame or at the location where you want to insert the picture in the document.

3. Choose File Import Picture.

   The Import Picture dialog box appears.

4. From the File Type list box, choose the file type. You can import graphics to Ami Pro in the following formats:

Format	File type
AmiDraw	SDW
AmiEquation	TEX
Computer Graphics Metafile	CGM
DrawPerfect	WPG
Encapsulated PostScript	EPS
Freelance	DRW
HP Graphic Language	HGL
Lotus 1-2-3 Graphics	PIC
PC Paintbrush	PCX
Scanned Images	TIF
Windows Bitmaps	BMP
Windows Metafile	WMF

5. From the Drives and Directories list boxes, specify the path for the graphic file you want to import.

6. From the Files list box, choose the graphic file you want to import.

7. If you want Ami Pro to use a copy of the image file instead of the original image file, choose the Copy Image check box. The image will display faster on-screen and will print faster because Ami Pro does not import the original file. Instead it imports a copy of the file.

8. Click OK or press Enter to insert the picture into the frame or at the insertion point.

Notes

To import graphics stored on the Clipboard, choose Edit Paste or press Shift+Ins.

To edit graphics, change colors, and insert callouts
and text, choose Tools Drawing to switch to Draw
mode. To use the Draw features, you must install
the AmiDraw program. For more information, refer
to *Using Ami Pro 3,* Special Edition.

Headers and Footers

Purpose

Prints information—such as chapter headings,
dates, or page numbers—below the top margin or
above the bottom margin of every page of a document. Header and footer information appears on-
screen in Layout mode.

To create a header or footer

1. Choose View Layout Mode to switch to Layout
   Mode view.

2. Choose Page Modify Page Layout.

   The Modify Page Layout dialog box appears.

3. From the Modify options, choose Header or
   Footer.

4. Choose the Begin on Second Page check box at
   the bottom of the Modify Page Layout dialog
   box.

   Usually headers and footers begin on the second page of the document.

5. Click OK or press Enter to confirm your choice
   and return to the document.

6. Place the insertion point in the upper or lower
   margin on any page in the document.

7. Type the text for the header or footer in the
   upper or lower margin.

Note

See also *Numbering Pages* and *View*.

Help

Purpose

Provides on-line, context-sensitive Help for any
function in Ami Pro. Help also enables you to learn
to use basic Ami Pro features and the new features
for upgraders. You can access Help at any time
while you are working on a document.

Help menu sections

The Help menu is divided into the following
sections:

Section	Purpose
Contents with Search and Browse	Provides an index to Help topics. You can search for specific topics or browse to find related topics.
Keyboard	Provides keyboard shortcuts for commands and functions.
How Do I?	Provides information about the common commands and functions you use in Ami Pro.
For Upgraders	Provides information on the improvements and new features in Ami Pro 3.
Enhancement Products	Provides information about other Windows programs you can use with Ami Pro 3.

To find a Help topic

1. Choose Help Index.

   The Help window appears.

2. You can use either of the following methods to find a Help topic:

   To find a Help topic using the Help Index, use the vertical scroll bar in the Help window or press ↑, ↓, PgUp, or PgDn to display more Help topics. Choose a topic by clicking the topic or pressing Tab to highlight the topic and then pressing Enter. Only underlined topics are available.

   To find a Help topic quickly, choose the Search button. The Search dialog box appears. Type a topic in the text box at the top of the dialog box, and then choose the Show Topics button to display a list of topics in the box at the bottom of the dialog box. Choose the topic you want to read, and then choose the Go To button to display information on the topic.

3. You can use the following techniques for moving between topics:

   To move to the preceding topic, choose the Back button in the Help window.

   To move to the preceding topic within a series of related topics, choose the << (Browse Backward) button in the Help window.

   To move to the next topic within a series of related topics, choose the >> (Browse Forward) button in the Help window.

4. To return to the Help Index, choose Index.

5. To display a list of the last fifty Help topics you viewed, choose the History button in the Help window.

   The History window displays a list of the last fifty Help topics in the order you viewed them.

6. To choose a topic you want to view again, double-click the topic. Or press ↑ or ↓ to highlight the topic, and then press Enter.

   The Help information appears in the Help window.

7. To print a Help topic, choose File Print Topic from the Help window.

8. To return to the document, choose File Exit from the Help window.

To use "What Is" Help

1. Press Shift+F1.

   A question mark pointer appears.

2. You can access information in the following ways:

   For more information about a menu command, place the question mark pointer on the command and click.

   For more information about a part of the screen, place the pointer on that part of the screen and double-click.

   For more information about a key or key combination, press the key or key combination.

   The information appears in the Help window.

Hyphenation

Purpose

Inserts a hyphen to divide a word that extends beyond the right margin of the page. The remainder of the hyphenated word wraps to the next line.

To hyphenate words automatically

1. Place the insertion point within a paragraph of text that uses the paragraph style for which you want to specify hyphenation.

2. Choose Style Modify Style.

   The Modify Style dialog box appears.

3. From the Modify options, choose the Hyphenation check box.

4. Choose OK or press Enter to begin hyphenation.

   Ami Pro hyphenates the appropriate words.

To override hyphenation for a particular word

1. Select the word you don't want to hyphenate.

2. Choose Edit Mark Text.

3. Choose No Hyphenation.

To specify hyphenation for a particular word

1. Place the insertion point at the location in the word where you want the discretionary hyphen.

2. Press Ctrl+- to insert the hyphen marker.

The Hyphenation Hot Zone

The *hyphenation hot zone* is the distance from the right margin within which the program hyphenates words.

To specify the hyphenation hot zone

1. Choose Tools User Setup.

   The User Setup dialog box appears.

2. Choose the Options button.

   The User Setup Options dialog box appears.

3. Enter the number of spaces (from two to nine) in the Hyphenation Hot-Zone box.

   If you specify a lower number for the Hyphenation Hot-Zone, more hyphens occur in the document and the margins appear less ragged.

   If you specify a higher number for the Hyphenation Hot-Zone, fewer hyphens occur in the document and the margins appear more ragged.

Indenting

Purpose

Aligns paragraphs relative to the margins.

To insert an indent

1. Place the insertion point in the paragraph you want to indent, or select the paragraphs you want to indent.

2. Choose Text Indentation.

   The Indentation dialog box appears.

3. Choose from the following Indentation options:

Option	Effect
All	Indents all lines from the left margin. Enter a positive or negative number to align the entire paragraph to the right or left of the left margin.
From Right	Indents all lines from the right margin. Enter a positive or negative number to align the entire paragraph to the right or left of the right margin.
First	Indents only the first line from the left margin in each paragraph. Enter a positive number in the text box to indent only the first line of the paragraph, or enter a negative number to create a hanging indent.
Rest	Indents all lines except the first line in each paragraph. Enter a positive number in the text box to indent all lines except the first line from the left margin to create a hanging indent.
Revert to Style	Restores the paragraph to the indent format in the existing style.

Note

See also *Ruler*.

Index

Purpose

Creates an index for a document. Ami Pro generates the page number references automatically.

To create an index entry

1. Use one of the following methods to form the index entry:

   Select the text (up to 64 characters) you want to use as an index entry.

   Place the insertion point where you want to create the index entry, type the index entry (up to 64 characters), and then select the index entry you typed.

2. Choose Edit Mark Text Index Entry.

   The Mark Index Entry dialog box appears. The index reference appears in the Primary text box.

3. In the Reference section, choose Page Number to display the entry with a page number.

4. Choose Other to place additional text and punctuation next to the entry in the index.

   If you want a comma or space between the index entry and the text, type the comma or space in the Other text box.

5. Choose the Mark button to close the Mark Index Entry dialog box and insert the index entry.

To index a recurring term

1. Choose Tools Macros Playback.

2. Choose the INDEXALL.SMM macro, and click OK or press Enter.

3. Select one occurrence of the term you want to mark for index entry.

4. Choose Edit Mark Text Mark Index All.

   Ami Pro marks every occurrence of the term as a primary index entry.

To mark an entry as a secondary entry

1. Cut the entry from the Primary text box.

2. Paste the entry into the Secondary text box.

To generate an index

1. Create the index entries and enter any formatting field codes.

2. Place the insertion point where you want the index to begin.

3. Choose the Tools TOC, Index command.

   The TOC, Index dialog box appears.

4. In the Generate area, choose Index.

5. Choose Include Alphabetical Separators to add a letter of the alphabet between sections.

6. In the Index Output File text box, enter the name of the file in which to generate the index.

   Otherwise, Ami Pro places the index in the same directory as the document being indexed.

7. In the Index Output File list box, specify the drive and directory for the index output file.

8. Click OK or press Enter to generate the index.

Ami Pro returns to the document, compiles the index, and then displays the index text and page numbers at the beginning of the document.

Note

See also *Table of Contents*.

Labels

Purpose

Creates mailing labels.

Before you can print labels, you use a mailing-label style sheet to create a label format, attach a data file, and then create a label layout.

To create a label format

1. Choose File New.

   The New dialog box appears.

2. From the Style Sheet for New Document list box, choose the LABEL style sheet.

3. Click OK or press Enter.

   The Labels dialog box appears.

4. From the Labels list box, choose the type of Avery or equivalent brand of mailing labels you use.

To create labels by merging

1. Choose the Merge button in the Labels dialog box.

   The Select Merge Data File dialog box appears.

2. From the Files list box, choose the data file that contains the fields you want to merge, and then click OK or press Enter.

   The Insert Merge Field dialog box appears.

3. From the Field Names list box, choose the field name you want to include on the label.

4. Choose Insert to paste the field name into the sample mailing label in the document.

5. Type the punctuation or paragraph mark you want to include after the mailing label text.

6. Repeat steps 3 through 5 to merge any other fields necessary to complete the layout for the mailing labels.

   If you make a mistake, make the corrections using the editing functions insert, delete, and typeover.

7. Choose the Continue Merge button.

   The Welcome to Merge dialog box appears.

8. Choose Option 3 to merge and print the data and the document, and then click OK or press Enter.

   The Merge dialog box appears.

9. Choose the Merge & Print option, and then click OK or press Enter to print the labels.

To create and print mailing labels manually

1. Choose the Manual button in the Labels dialog box.

   Ami Pro displays a table that represents the label format.

2. Type the label text in each cell.

   Use the Tab key to move to a cell.

3. Choose File Print.

   The Print dialog box appears.

4. Specify any Print options you want.

5. Click OK or press Enter.

   The mailing labels print.

Notes

After you create a label format with the mailing-label style sheet, you can print sets of mailing labels by opening the main document that contains the label format and choosing the File Merge command.

See also *Merge*.

Line Spacing

Purpose

Adjusts line spacing to improve the appearance of a document.

To adjust line spacing

1. Select the text for which you want to adjust line spacing.

2. Choose Text Spacing.

   The Spacing dialog box appears.

3. Choose one of the following Spacing options:

Option	Effect
Single	Specifies single spacing; adds no additional space between lines; the default setting.

Option	Effect
1 1/2	Specifies 1 1/2-line spacing; adds 1/2 line of additional space between lines.
Double	Specifies double spacing; adds one line of additional space between lines.
Custom	Specifies the amount of space you want between lines. Type the number of lines in the Custom text box, or click the arrows next to the Custom text box to change the number of lines to a different number.
Revert to Style	Restores the paragraph to the spacing format in the existing style.

4. Click **OK** or press **Enter** to adjust the spacing.

Note

See also *Styles*.

Purpose

Links data from another application to an Ami Pro document. If you change the data in the other application, Ami Pro updates the linked data in the Ami Pro document.

To create a link

1. Start the application and open the file that contains the data you want to link to an Ami Pro document.

2. Select the data you want to link to an Ami Pro document.

3. Choose Edit Copy to copy the data to the Clipboard.

   Do not close the application.

4. Start Ami Pro and choose File Open to open the document with which you want to create the link.

5. Place the insertion point in the Ami Pro document where you want to create the link.

6. Choose Edit Paste Link for DDE applications, or choose Edit Paste Special for OLE applications. DDE (Dynamic Data Exchange) is a Microsoft utility that connects applications that support DDE. OLE (Object Linking and Embedding) is a Microsoft utility that connects applications and lets you choose the format for the object you paste into Ami Pro.

   Windows inserts the linked data in the Ami Pro document.

To update linked data

1. Keep the other application open when you want to update the Ami Pro document.

2. Choose File Open to reopen the Ami Pro document.

3. Choose Edit Link Options.

   The Link Options dialog box appears.

4. Choose Update to update the linked data.

Notes

You also can edit an existing link or modify link options using the Edit Link Options command.

Ami Pro can link to other Windows applications that support DDE or OLE, including worksheet files and charts created in Lotus 1-2-3 for Windows, and to picture and bit-mapped files from Lotus Freelance for Windows.

Lists

Purpose

Creates bulleted or numbered lists.

To create a bulleted list

1. Choose Style Create Style from the menu bar.

   The Create Style dialog box appears.

2. Type the name of the new paragraph style in the New Style text box.

3. Choose the Modify button.

   The Modify Style dialog box appears.

4. From the Modify options, choose the Bullets & Numbers option.

5. Choose the Bullet check box.

6. From the Bullet list box, choose a bullet symbol.

7. In the Space For text box, specify the amount of space to indent the text following the bullet.

8. Click OK or press Enter.

9. Select the paragraphs you want to appear as bulleted lists.

10. From the menu bar, choose Style Select a Style.

   A dialog box appears containing a list of styles.

11. Choose the new bullet style.

12. Click OK or press Enter.

To create a numbered list

1. Choose Style Create Style from the menu bar.

   The Create Style dialog box appears.

2. Type the name of the new paragraph style in the New Style text box.

3. Choose the Modify button.

   The Modify Style dialog box appears.

4. From the Modify options, choose the Bullets & Numbers option.

5. Choose the Number check box.

6. From the Number list box, choose numbers, roman numerals, or letters.

7. In the Space For text box, specify the amount of space to indent the text following the number.

8. Click OK or press Enter.

9. Select the paragraphs you want to appear as bulleted lists.

10. From the menu bar, choose Style Select a Style.

   A dialog box appears containing a list of styles.

11. Choose the new numbered list style.

12. Click OK or press Enter.

To delete a list item

1. Select the list item you want to remove.

2. Press Del to remove the text.

   In a numbered list, Ami Pro renumbers the list.

Note

See also *Styles*.

Macros

Purpose

Records a sequence of keystrokes you can play back later. Macros enable you to automate Ami Pro keystrokes, but not mouse actions.

To record a macro

1. Choose Tools Macros Record.

   The Record Macro dialog box appears.

2. In the Macro File text box, type a file name for the macro.

3. In the Playback Shortcut Keys text box, press the key or keys you want to use as a shortcut.

   You can use a function key, Ctrl with a function key, Shift with a function key, or both Ctrl and Shift with a function key.

4. Click OK or press Enter to record the macro.

   Recording Macro appears on the status bar to indicate that you are recording.

5. Choose the Ami Pro menu commands and other keystrokes you want to include in the macro.

6. When you finish recording the macro, choose Tools Macros End Record.

To run a macro

Press the shortcut key combination for the macro.

To run a macro by using menu commands

1. Choose Tools Macros Playback.

   The Play Macro dialog box appears.

2. Choose the macro you want to run from the Macros list box.

3. Click OK or press Enter to run the macro.

To assign a macro to a file so that it runs automatically

1. Open the file to which you want to assign a macro.

2. Choose Tools Macros Edit.

   The Edit Macro dialog box appears.

3. Choose the Assign button.

   The Assign Macro to Run Automatically dialog box appears.

4. From the Run Macro options, choose the File Open option to run the macro when the file is opened, or choose the File Close option to run the macro when the file is closed.

   You also can choose both options.

5. Choose the macro you want to assign to the file from the File Open or File Close list box, or from both list boxes.

6. Click OK or press Enter to return to the Edit Macro dialog box.

7. Click OK or press Enter to return to the document.

   You now can run the macro when you open or close the file.

To assign a macro to a SmartIcon

1. Choose Tools SmartIcons.

   The SmartIcons dialog box appears.

2. Choose the Edit Icon button.

   The Edit SmartIcon dialog box appears.

3. From the Available Icons list box, choose the SmartIcon to which you want to assign the macro.

   The SmartIcon appears in the example area in the dialog box.

4. In the Macros list box, choose the macro you want to assign to the SmartIcon.

5. Click OK or press Enter to return to the SmartIcons dialog box.

6. Click OK or press Enter to close the SmartIcons dialog box.

   You now can choose the macro from the SmartIcon set.

Note

See also *SmartIcons*.

Margins

Purpose

Adjusts the left, right, top, and bottom margins.

To set margins by using the Modify Page Layout command

1. Choose View Layout Mode to switch to Layout mode.

2. Choose Page Modify Page Layout.

   The Modify Page Layout dialog box appears.

3. From the Modify options, choose the Margins & Columns option.

4. Type new margin measurements in the Left, Right, Top, and Bottom text boxes.

5. Click OK or press Enter to set the margins.

To set margins using the Ruler in the Modify Page Layout dialog box

1. Choose View Layout Mode to switch to Layout mode.

2. Choose Page Modify Page Layout.

   The Modify Page Layout dialog box appears.

3. From the Modify options, choose the Margins & Columns option.

   The Ruler appears at the top of the dialog box.

4. Drag the margin markers (left arrow and right arrow in the bottom half of the Ruler) along the Ruler to set the new margins.

To set margins using the Ruler

1. Choose View Show Ruler.

   The Ruler appears at the top of the document window.

2. Place the insertion point where you want to change the margins, or select the text for which you want to adjust the margins.

3. Drag the margin markers (left arrow and right arrow in the bottom half of the Ruler) along the Ruler to set the new margins.

Note

See also *Page Layout* and *Ruler*.

Master Document

Purpose

Organizes large writing projects by combining multiple documents into one master document. A master document contains codes linking the master to the individual documents.

You can generate indexes, tables of contents, and consecutive page numbering for the master document and still work on the individual documents.

To create a master document

1. Choose File Master Document.

   The Master Document dialog box appears.

2. In the Directories list box, specify the drive and directory of the first file you want to include in the master document.

3. From the File list box, choose the first file you want to include in the master document.

4. Choose the Include button.

   The file name appears in the Master Doc Files list box.

5. Repeat steps 2 through 4 to specify the other files you want to include in the master document.

6. Click OK or press Enter.

To delete a document from the master document

Choose the file from the File list box, and choose the Remove button.

The file name no longer appears in the Master Doc Files list box.

To create a table of contents for a master document

1. Choose File Master Document.

   The Master Document dialog box appears.

2. Choose the Options button.

   The Master Document Options dialog box appears.

3. Choose the Generate TOC check box.

4. In the Output File text box, type the name of the file in which to generate the table of contents.

5. To specify TOC options, choose the TOC Options button and choose any options you want. Then click OK or press Enter to return to the Master Document Options dialog box.

6. Click OK or press Enter to return to the Master Document dialog box.

7. Click OK or press Enter to return to the Master Document file.

   Ami Pro generates the table of contents.

8. From the menu bar, choose Tools TOC, Index.

   The TOC Index dialog box appears.

9. Under the Generate options, mark the Table of Contents check box.

10. Click OK or press Enter.

To create an index for a master document

1. Choose File Master Document.

   The Master Document dialog box appears.

2. Choose the Options button.

   The Master Document Options dialog box appears.

3. Choose the Generate Index check box.

4. Choose the Include Alphabetical Separators check box to add a letter of the alphabet between sections.

5. In the Output File text box, type the name of the file in which to generate the index.

6. Click OK or press Enter to return to the Master Document file.

7. From the menu bar, choose Tools TOC, Index.

   The TOC Index dialog box appears.

8. Under the Generate options, mark the Index check box.

9. Click OK or press Enter.

   Ami Pro generates the index.

Note

See also *Index* and *Table of Contents*.

Merge

Purpose

Combines two files into one file, inserting variable data into a fixed format.

Before you can merge files, you must create two files—the *data file* and the *merge document file*. The data file contains the variable information, such as names and addresses, you merge into the main document file. The merge document file contains field names and the information that remains constant. Each field name corresponds to a field name in the data file.

To create a data file

1. Choose File Merge.

   The Welcome to Merge dialog box appears.

2. Choose Option 1, Select, Create, or Edit a Data File, to create a data file.

   The Print Merge Setup dialog box appears.

3. Click OK or press Enter.

   The Select Merge Data File dialog box appears.

4. Choose the New button.

   The Create Data File dialog box appears.

5. In the Field Name box, type the name of the first field.

   Do not enter a space after the field name.

6. Choose the Add button or press Enter.

   The first field name appears in the Fields in Data File box.

7. Type the next field name, and then choose the Add button or press Enter.

   Repeat this step for each field you want to include in the data file.

8. After you enter all the fields, click OK to save the information.

9. Type a name for the data file in the File Name text box.

10. Click OK or press Enter to save the data file.

    Ami Pro inserts the field names and record delimiters (~|) on the first line of the merge data file.

    The Data File dialog box (which looks like an index card) appears. The field names you entered appear in the dialog box.

To enter information in the data file

1. Type the information in the text box for the first field of the first record.

2. Press Tab to move to the next field, or click the text box for the next field.

3. Type the information for the next field.

4. Repeat steps 2 and 3 to enter information in the first record's remaining fields.

5. At the end of the record, choose the Add button to create a new, blank record.

   The first ten characters of the record's first field appear in a tab divider at the top of the dialog box.

6. Repeat steps 1 through 5 to enter the information for each record in the data file.

7. When you finish entering all the records, choose Close.

   Ami Pro prompts you to save the file.

8. Choose Yes to save the information in the data file.

   The Save As dialog box appears.

9. Type a file name in the File Name text box.

10. Click OK or press Enter to save the data file.

To create a merge document file

After you save the data file, Ami Pro displays the New dialog box.

1. Click OK or press Enter to create a new file for the merge document.

   The Welcome to Merge dialog box appears.

2. Choose Option 2, Create or Edit a Merge Document, to create a merge document file.

   Ami Pro asks you whether you want to use the current file as the merge document file.

3. Choose Yes or press Enter.

   The Insert Merge Field dialog box appears.

4. Create the format (margins, line spacing, fonts, and so on) you want to use in the merge document (see *Styles* and *Page Layout*).

5. Type any text you want to appear before the field of a record. For example, type Dear for the salutation that will appear before the Name field.

6. Place the insertion point where you want the field to begin.

7. From the Field Names list box, choose the field name you want to insert.

8. Choose the Insert button to paste the field name into the document.

9. Repeat steps 5 through 8 until you complete the document.

   Add any necessary spacing and punctuation before and after the fields.

10. Choose Close to close the Insert Merge field dialog box and return to the merge document.

11. Save the merge document file.

To merge the merge document and data files

1. Choose File Merge.

   The Welcome to Merge dialog box appears.

2. Choose Option 3, Merge and Print the Data and the Document, to merge and print the merge document and data files.

3. Click OK or press Enter.

   The Merge dialog box appears.

4. Choose the Merge & Print option.

5. Click OK or press Enter to merge the merge document and data files.

   The Print Merge Setup dialog box appears.

6. Click OK or press Enter.

   Ami Pro prints one copy of the main document for each record in the data file.

Notes

Each type of item in a data file, such as the first name, is a *field*. All fields that belong together, such as the name and address of one person, comprise a *record*.

You can enter as many fields in a record as you want, but each record in a data file must have the same number of fields, even if some fields are blank. The fields must be in the same order in each record.

To display the field codes in the main document, choose the View Show Power Fields command.

Notes

Purpose

Inserts comments and reminders, called *notes*, into a document. *Note marks* identify each note with your initials and a number.

Ami Pro hides notes unless you choose to display them. You can print the notes with the document, including an index of the document's notes, your initials, and the note numbers.

To insert a note

1. Place the insertion point where you want to insert the note.

2. Choose Edit Insert Note.

   The Note window appears.

   Ami Pro inserts your initials from the User Setup dialog box, and numbers the annotation in the order in which the notes occur in the document.

3. Type the text of the annotation in the Note window.

4. Choose the Control menu, and then choose the Close button to return to the document.

To display or hide note marks

1. Choose View View Preferences.

2. Choose the Notes check box to display the note markers in the text, with note rectangles.

   Turn off the Notes check box to hide the note rectangles that represent the notes.

3. Click OK or press Enter to close the dialog box and return to the document.

To view notes by clicking with the mouse

Double-click the note mark in the text.

The Note window appears.

To view notes by using commands

1. Choose Edit Go To or press Ctrl+G.

   The Go To dialog box appears.

2. Choose the Next Item option in the Go To dialog box.

3. In the Next Item list box, choose Note.

4. Choose the Go To ^H button or press Enter to view the next note that occurs in the text.

   The Note window appears.

5. After reading the note, choose the Control menu and choose Close to close the Note window and return to the document.

To view a document's next note using a keyboard shortcut

Press Ctrl+H to view the next note in a document.

To remove a note

1. Choose the Control menu in the Note window.

    The Control menu appears.

2. Choose Remove This Note to remove the current note, or choose Remove All Notes to remove all notes in the document.

To print the document and notes

1. Choose File Print or press Ctrl+P.

    The Print dialog box appears.

2. Choose the Options button.

    The Print Options dialog box appears.

3. From the Print Options area, choose the With Notes check box.

4. Click OK or press Enter to close the Print Options dialog box.

5. Choose any other Print options (see *Print*).

6. Click OK or press Enter to print the document and notes.

    The initials and note number enclosed in brackets print at the location of the note in the text. The complete notes, initials, and note numbers print on a separate page at the end of the document text.

Numbering Lines

Purpose

Numbers lines in a document automatically. If you move lines, Ami Pro updates the line numbers to reflect the new line order.

To number lines

1. Open the document you want to line number.

2. Choose Page Line Numbering.

   The Line Numbering dialog box appears.

3. You can use any of the following Line Numbering options:

   To specify the type of line numbering, choose
   Number All Lines or Number Text Lines from
   the list box at the top of the dialog box.

   To specify the increment for line numbers,
   choose one of the Line Numbering options.

   To restart line numbers at the top of each
   page, choose the Reset Each Page check box.

   To specify a particular style for the line numbers, choose a style from the Based On list
   box.

4. Click OK or press Enter to insert the line
   numbers in the document.

To remove line numbers

1. Open the document from which you want to
   remove line numbers.

2. Choose Page Line Numbering.

   The Line Numbering dialog box appears.

3. From the list box at the top of the dialog box,
   choose None.

4. Click OK or press Enter to remove the line
   numbers.

Numbering Pages

Purpose

Numbers pages automatically and prints the page numbers in the location you specify.

To number pages

1. Place the insertion point in the top or bottom margin on any page.

2. Choose **P**age **P**age Numbering.

   The Page Numbering dialog box appears.

3. From the **S**tyle list box, choose numbers, Roman numerals, or letters.

4. You can use the following options for alternative ways to start the page numbering:

   If you want to start numbering pages on a page other than the first page, choose the Start on **P**age check box and specify the page number with which to start numbering pages.

   If you want to start numbering pages with a number other than one, choose the Start with **N**umber check box and specify the number with which to start numbering pages.

5. Click **OK** or press **Enter** to number the pages.

Open

Purpose

Opens a file in a document window.

To open a file

1. Choose File Open or press Ctrl+O.

2. If the file you want to open is not listed in the Files list box, you can use the following techniques:

   If the file you want to open is on another drive, choose the drive name from the Drives list box.

   If the file you want to open is in another directory, choose the directory name from the Directories list box.

   The list of files in the chosen directory appears in the Files list box.

3. Double-click the name of the file you want to open. Or press ↓ to highlight the name of the file you want to open, and then press Enter.

Notes

To open a file quickly, click the Open SmartIcon on the SmartIcons set.

See also *SmartIcons*.

Outlines

Purpose

Creates outline structures upon which you build an outline of a document. If you move elements of the outline to another position in the document, Ami Pro renumbers the elements for you.

To create an outline

1. Place the insertion point where you want the outline to begin.

2. Choose View Outline Mode.

   The Outline set appears at the top of the document. The Outline command appears in the menu bar.

3. Type the text for the first heading and press Enter.

   Ami Pro inserts a first-level heading.

4. To enter another heading in the document that is the same level as the preceding heading, type the text for the new heading and press Enter.

   To enter a heading that is one level below the preceding heading (indented to the right of the preceding heading), you *demote* the heading level.

   To demote a heading level, press Alt+→ or click the Demote icon (right arrow with a circle) on the Outline set. Then type the heading.

   A demoted heading level is sometimes called a *subordinate level*.

   To enter a heading level that is one level higher than the preceding heading (moved to the left of the preceding heading), you *promote* the heading level.

   To promote a heading level, press Alt+← or click the Promote icon (left arrow with a circle) on the Outline set. Then type the heading.

   A promoted heading level is sometimes called a *superior level*.

5. Use the following methods to move levels higher or lower:

   To move a heading to a higher level, press Alt+↑ or click the Move Up icon (up arrow with a square) on the Outline set.

   To move a heading to a lower level, press Alt+↓ or click the Move Down icon (down arrow with a square) on the Outline set.

Note

To display an outline and view the numbered levels, use the outline feature in a blank document.

Page Breaks

Purpose

Inserts page breaks (where you want one page to end and another page to begin) in documents.

Ami Pro has two kinds of page breaks—*soft* and *hard*. Whenever you fill a page of text, Ami Pro inserts a soft page break. If you add or delete text, any soft page breaks move accordingly.

To insert a page break in a specific location, you manually insert a hard page break. Hard page breaks remain in the same location, even when you add or delete text.

To insert a hard page break

1. Place the insertion point where you want to end one page and begin another.

2. Choose Page Breaks.

   The Breaks dialog box appears.

3. Choose the Insert Page Break option.

4. Click OK or press Enter to insert the page break.

To find a hard page break

1. Choose Edit Go To or press Ctrl+G.

2. Choose the Next Item option.

3. Choose Hard Pg Break in the Next Item list box.

4. Choose the Go To ^H button to move to the next hard page break in the document.

5. Repeat steps 1 through 4 until you find the page break you want to delete.

To delete a hard page break

1. Choose Page Breaks.

   The Breaks dialog box appears.

2. Choose the Remove Page Break option.

3. Click OK or press Enter to remove the page break.

To control page breaks within paragraphs

1. Select the paragraphs you do not want Ami Pro to divide with a soft page break.

2. Choose Style Modify Style.

   The Modify Style dialog box appears.

3. From the Modify options, choose the Breaks option.

4. Choose one of the following Breaks options:

Option	Effect
Page Break Before Paragraph	Inserts a page break before the paragraph so that the paragraph appears at the top of the next page.
Page Break After Paragraph	Inserts a page break after the paragraph so that the paragraph appears at the bottom of the previous page.
Allow Page/Column Break Within	Keeps all the lines of the paragraph on the same page.

5. If you want to keep paragraphs on the same page, instead of using the Breaks options, choose one of the following Keep With options:

Option	Effect
Previous Paragraph	Keeps that paragraph and the previous paragraph on the same page.
Next Paragraph	Keeps that paragraph and the next paragraph on the same page.

6. Click OK or press Enter to return to the document.

Notes

To see the effect of the page breaks in a document, choose the View Layout Mode command.

See also *Page Layout*.

Page Layout

Purpose

Enables you to change the layout of a page by setting margins and tabs, setting up columns, choosing paper size and page orientation, inserting lines and borders, and customizing headers and footers.

To set or change the page layout

1. Place the insertion point at the beginning of the document for which you want to change the page layout, or at the location where you want to change the page layout.

2. Choose Page Modify Page Layout.

   The Modify Page Layout dialog box appears.

3. Choose from the following Modify options:

Option	Effect
Margins & Columns	Specifies tab and margin settings; sets up columns and the space between columns.
Page Settings	Specifies the paper size and page orientation. Choose Letter, Legal, A4, A3, A5, or B5; or specify a custom paper size by choosing Custom and

Option	Effect
	entering the width and length in the Custom text boxes. Choose Portrait or Landscape to specify the page orientation.
Lines	Draws lines around the page. Choose All, Left, Right, Top, or Bottom to specify the placement of the lines. Choose Inside, Close to Inside, Middle, Close to Outside, or Outside to specify the position of the lines on the page. Choose a line style from the Around Page and Position Style list box. To specify a line between columns, choose the Line Between Columns check box, and choose a line style from the Line Between Columns Style list box. Choose a color from the color bar to specify a color for the lines.
Header	Specifies margins, columns, and tabs within the header. Enables you to begin the header on the second page. Choose the Begin on Second Page check box.
Footer	Specifies margins, columns, and tabs within the footer. Enables you to begin the footer on the second page. Choose the Begin on Second Page check box.

4. Choose from the following Pages options:

Option	Effect
All	Specifies page layout settings for all pages in the document.
Right	Specifies page layout settings for the right pages in the document.
Left	Specifies page layout settings for the left pages in the document.
Mirror	Specifies the same page layout settings for both the right and left pages, but reverses them. Choose the Right or Left option, and then choose Mirror to use a mirror image of the right page layout settings for the left pages or use a mirror image of the left page layout settings for the right pages.

5. Click OK or press Enter to return to the document.

Notes

To see the effect of the page layout changes in a document, choose the View Layout Mode command.

See also *Columns, Frames, Headers and Footers, Margins,* and *Tabs.*

Password Protection

Purpose

Assigns a password to a document. A password limits access to the document to users who know the password.

> **CAUTION:** Use passwords with caution. Ami Pro will not open a password-protected file unless you enter the correct password.

To set a password

1. Choose File Save As.

   The Save As dialog box appears.

   If you have not named the document, type a name in the File Name text box.

2. Choose the Password Protect check box.

3. Click OK or press Enter to close the Save As dialog box.

   The Password Protect dialog box appears.

4. In the Enter Password text box, type a password—up to 14 characters, including spaces, in uppercase or lowercase letters.

   The password appears as a series of asterisks.

5. Click OK or press Enter to enter the password.

   The Password Protect verification dialog box appears.

6. In the Verify Password text box, type the password again to verify it.

    The password appears as asterisks again.

7. Click OK or press Enter to save the document with password protection.

To remove a password

1. Choose File Save As.

    The Save As dialog box appears.

2. Choose the Password Protect check box.

3. Click OK or press Enter to close the Save As dialog box.

    The Password Protect dialog box appears.

4. Press Del to delete the password.

5. Click OK or press Enter to save the change and return to the Save As dialog box.

6. Click OK or press Enter to save the document without password protection.

Note

See also *Save/Save As*.

Paste

Purpose

Inserts the Clipboard's contents in a specified location in the same document, in another document, or in a document in another Windows program.

To paste data

1. Open the document that contains the text you want to paste and the document where you want to paste that data.

2. Cut or copy the data to the Clipboard.

3. Place the insertion point where you want to insert the Clipboard's contents.

   If you want to paste the data in another document, or in a document in another Windows program, choose the Window menu and then choose the document where you want to paste data.

4. Choose Edit Paste or press Ctrl+V.

   A copy of the Clipboard's contents appears in the document. The data also remains on the Clipboard until you cut or copy something else or exit Windows.

Notes

To choose the Cut, Copy, or Paste command quickly, you can click the Cut, Copy, or Paste SmartIcon on the SmartIcons set.

See also *Clipboard, Copy, Cut,* and *SmartIcons.*

Power Fields

Purpose

Enables you to automate document production. A power field contains instructions for performing routine actions in Ami Pro. You can insert dates or page numbers, prompt the user to enter data, create your own error messages, and much more.

To use predefined power fields

1. Place the insertion point where you want to insert a power field.

2. Choose Edit Power Fields Insert.

   The Insert Power Fields dialog box appears.

3. In the Fields list box, choose the power field you want to insert.

   The power field appears in the Insert text box.

4. To specify a format for the power field, choose a format from the Options list box.

5. Click OK or press Enter to insert the power field.

6. To display the power fields in the document, choose View Show Power Fields.

Print

Purpose

Prints a document using the printer and font settings you choose.

To print a document

1. Open the document you want to print.

2. Choose File Print or press Ctrl+P.

   The Print dialog box appears.

3. Choose from the following Print options:

Option	Effect
Number of Copies	Specifies the number of copies you want to print.
Page Range	Specifies the range of pages you want to print.
Including	Prints Even Pages, Odd Pages, or Both even and odd pages.

4. To specify other Print options, choose the Options button.

   The Print Options dialog box appears.

5. Choose from the following Print options:

Option	Effect
Reverse Order	Prints the document in reverse order. The last page is printed first.
Collate	Prints a complete copy of the document before the next copy of the document begins to print.
Crop Marks	Prints crop marks a half inch outside the document margins. Useful for trimming the page.
Without Pictures	Prints only the document text; does not print pictures.
With Notes	Prints the initials and number at the location of the note within the

Option	Effect
	document and prints the note text at the end of the document.
With Doc Description	Prints the document description as the cover page for the document.
On Preprinted Form	Prints the document on a preprinted form without protected text, lines, shading, or tables.
Update Fields	Prints the information referenced by power fields.
Bin Options	Specifies which printer bin you want to use for the First Page of the document and the Rest of the document.

6. Click OK or press Enter to close the Print Options dialog box and return to the Print dialog box.

7. Click OK or press Enter to print the document.

Notes

To print a document immediately, click the Print SmartIcon on the SmartIcons set.

If you choose the Collate check box, Ami Pro creates the specified number of copies and then sends all the copies of the document to the printer. This option produces collated copies, but printing takes longer.

See also *Notes*, *Printer Setup*, *Protecting Text*, and *View*.

Printer Setup

Purpose

Chooses a printer, switches printers, changes printer settings, chooses cartridges and fonts, and chooses a paper source.

To choose a printer or change printer settings

1. Choose File Printer Setup.

   The Select Printer dialog box appears.

2. From the Printer for This Document list box, choose the printer you want to use.

3. To change printer settings, choose the Setup button.

   The Printer dialog box appears.

   The settings in the dialog box vary depending on the chosen printer. Usually, graphics resolution, printer model, color, orientation, paper feed, text mode, and paper width and height settings are available.

4. Change the settings, and then click OK or press Enter to accept the settings and return to the Select Printer dialog box.

5. Click OK or press Enter to accept the printer selection and setup and to return to the document.

Protecting Text

Purpose

Protects text from modifications.

To protect text

1. Select the text you want to protect.
2. Choose Edit Mark Text Protected Text.

To unprotect text

1. Select the protected text you want to unprotect using the **Shift** key and the arrow keys.
2. Choose Edit Mark Text Protected Text.

Note

See also *Password Protection*.

Revision Marks

Purpose

Indicates changes to a document by displaying revision bars in the margins and by using formatted characters for inserted text and strikethrough characters for deleted text.

Ami Pro uses the Revision Marking options you set to compare an edited document to the original document when you use the Tools Doc Compare command (see *Comparing Documents*).

To display revision marks

1. Open the document in which you want to mark changes.
2. Choose Tools Revision Marking.

   The Revision Marking dialog box appears.

3. Choose the Mark Revisions check box.

4. Choose the Options button.

   The Revision Marking Options dialog box appears.

5. From the Mark Insertions As options, choose a character format for inserted text.

   The default character format is Italic.

6. From the Mark Deletions As options, choose a character format for deleted text.

   The default character format is Strikethrough.

7. Choose one of the following options for revision marks in the margin:

Option	Effect
None	Does not display revision bars.
Revision Bars	Displays revision bars (vertical lines) in the margin (the feature's default setting).
Revision Character	Displays a character in the margin. Type the character in the Revision Character text box.

8. Choose one of the following options for positioning revision marks in the margin:

Option	Effect
Left	Displays and prints revision bars in the left margin in Layout Mode view and when you use the Tools Doc Compare command.

Option	Effect
Right	Displays and prints revision bars in the right margin in Layout Mode View and when you use the Tools Doc Compare command.
Rt/Left	Displays and prints revision bars in the left margin on even pages and in the right margin on odd pages.

9. Click OK or press Enter to save your choices and return to the Revision Marking dialog box.

10. Click OK or press Enter to return to the document.

    The REV indicator appears in the status bar.

To use revision marks

Add text to the existing text. The text you add has the character format you specified in the Revision Marks dialog box. The default character format is Italic.

Delete text by choosing Edit Cut, pressing Del, or clicking the Cut SmartIcon on the SmartIcons set. The text you delete changes to the character format you specified in the Revision Marks dialog box. The default character format is Strikethrough.

To hide revision marks

1. Choose Tools Revision Marking.

    The Revision Marking dialog box appears.

2. Choose the Mark Revisions check box.

3. Turn off the Mark Revisions check box by choosing it again.

4. Click OK or press Enter to return to the document.

To review revisions

1. Choose Tools Revision Marking.

   The Revision Marking dialog box appears.

2. Choose the Review Rev button.

   Ami Pro finds the first revision mark.

3. To find the next revision mark, choose the Review Rev button again.

   To stop the search, choose Cancel.

4. Use the following methods to accept revisions:

   To accept insertion revisions, choose the Accept This Insertion button. Ami Pro removes the revision marks.

   To accept deletion revisions, choose the Accept This Deletion button. The program deletes the marked text.

   To accept revisions for the entire document, choose the Accept All Rev button in the Revision Marking dialog box.

5. Use the following methods to reject revisions:

   To reject insertion revisions, choose the Cancel This Insertion button.

   To reject deletion revisions, choose the Cancel This Deletion button.

   To reject revisions for the entire document, choose the Cancel All Rev button in the Revision Marking dialog box.

Ami Pro removes the revision marks and undoes the marked revisions. The original text
remains intact.

Ruler

Purpose

Changes character and paragraph formats quickly.
You can use the Ruler to set tabs and margins,
format text, and adjust columns and tables.

To display or hide the Ruler

To display the Ruler, choose View Show Ruler.

To hide the Ruler, choose View Show Ruler again.

To set a tab

1. Select the text for which you want to set a tab,
   or place the insertion point where you want
   the new tabs to begin.

2. Click the Ruler.

   The Tab bar appears below the Ruler.

3. Click one of the tab buttons (Left, Right,
   Numeric, or Center) on the Tab bar, and then
   click the top half of the Ruler where you want
   to add the tab.

   The tab marker (a blue arrow with or without a
   vertical line and a decimal point) indicates the
   position of the tab.

To change a tab

1. Select the text for which you want to change a tab, or place the insertion point where you want to change a tab.

2. Use the appropriate technique from the following list:

   To adjust the position of an existing tab, drag the tab marker to the new position.

   To delete an existing tab, drag the tab marker off the Ruler and release the mouse button.

   To change the type of tab, delete the existing tab. Then click a tab button on the Tab bar and click the Ruler where you want to add the new tab.

To reset the left and right margins

The *margin markers* (black arrows) appear on the bottom half of the Ruler, one at each end.

Drag the margin markers to the new positions.

To indent paragraphs

1. Select the paragraphs you want to indent.

2. Click on the Ruler.

   The *indentation markers* (vertical bar and blue arrows) appear on the top half of the Ruler.

3. Use the appropriate technique from the following list:

   To indent the entire paragraph to the left, drag the all indentation marker (the vertical bar at the left end of the Ruler) to the new position.

To indent the entire paragraph to the right, drag the right indentation marker (the large arrow at the right end of the Ruler) to the new position.

To indent only the first line of the paragraph, drag the first-line indentation marker (the top arrow at the left end of the Ruler) to the new position.

To create a hanging indent, drag the rest indentation marker (the bottom arrow at the left end of the Ruler) to the new position, drag the first-line indentation marker (the top arrow at the left end of the Ruler) to the new position, and drag the all indentation marker (the vertical bar at the left end of the Ruler) to the new position.

To adjust column width

Before you can adjust column width on the Ruler, you must use the Page Modify Page Layout command to set up the columns.

The column margin markers (black arrows) appear on the bottom half of the Ruler in groups of two for each column.

Drag the margin markers to the new positions.

Notes

You can use the Page Modify Page Layout command to change margin and tab settings on the Ruler in the Modify Page Layout dialog box.

You can insert a ruler anywhere in a document to create different tab, indent, or margin settings for particular pages or paragraphs. To insert a ruler, choose **P**age **R**uler **I**nsert. To delete a ruler, choose **P**age **R**uler **R**emove.

See also *Columns*, *Margins*, *Page Layout*, *Tables*, and *Tabs*.

Save/Save As

Purpose

Saves an existing document (Save), a new document, or an existing document with a different name, in a different format, or in a different directory (Save As).

To save a document

1. Choose **F**ile **S**ave or **F**ile Save **A**s, or press **Ctrl+S** (Save).

   If you are saving a previously saved document and you choose the **F**ile **S**ave command, Ami Pro saves the document.

   If you have not saved the document previously or you choose the **F**ile Save **A**s command, the Save As dialog box appears.

2. Choose from the following Save As options:

   To save the document on a different drive, choose a drive from the Dri**v**es list box.

   To save the document in a different directory, choose a directory from the **D**irectories list box.

To name the document or to save the document with a different name, type the name in
the File Name text box.

To save the document in a different format,
choose a format from the List Files As Type
list box.

3. Click OK or press Enter to save the new file.

Notes

The File Save command replaces the original copy
of a document (the file on your drive) with the
document on-screen. The File Save As command
enables you to rename the document on-screen so
that you can retain the earlier version as well as
save your changes.

If you try to close a document without saving it, Ami
Pro asks whether you want to save the document.

You also can click the Save SmartIcon on the
SmartIcons set rather than choose the File Save
command.

See also *SmartIcons* and *Convert File*.

SmartIcons

Purpose

Chooses commands, features, and options quickly.
Ami Pro provides a default SmartIcon set, but you
can display other SmartIcon sets. You can customize any SmartIcon set with buttons for frequently
used commands.

The default SmartIcon set contains the following
SmartIcons:

Button	Name	Effect
	Open	Opens a file.
	Save	Saves a file.
	Print	Prints a document.
	Print Envelope	Sets up and prints an address for an envelope.
	Full Page/ Layout View	Toggles between Full Page View and Layout Mode View.
	Undo	Undoes the preceding action.
	Cut	Cuts text.
	Copy	Copies text.
	Paste	Pastes text.
	Bold	Bolds text.
	Italic	Italicizes text.
	Underline	Underlines text.
	Fast Format	Sets up Fast Format.
	Left Align	Left aligns text.
	Center Align	Centers text.

Button	Name	Effect
	Hide/Show Ruler	Toggles between hiding and displaying the Ruler.
	Frame	Inserts a frame.
	Table	Inserts a table.
	Spell Check	Checks the spelling in a document.
	Thesaurus	Finds synonyms and definitions for a word in a document.
	Grammar Check	Checks the punctuation, grammar, and style in a document.
	Draw	Starts AmiDraw.
	Chart	Enables you to create a chart in a document.
	Next Icon Set	Displays the next SmartIcons set.
	Floating/Fixed SmartIcons	Toggles between floating SmartIcons and fixed SmartIcons.

To display or hide the default SmartIcon set

To display the SmartIcons set, choose the Hide/
Show SmartIcons button in the status bar. Then
choose Show SmartIcons from the list.

To hide the SmartIcons set, choose the Hide/Show SmartIcons button in the status bar. Then choose Hide SmartIcons from the list.

To use a SmartIcon on the SmartIcon set

Click the SmartIcon you want to use. You must have a mouse to use the SmartIcon set.

To delete a SmartIcon from the SmartIcon set

1. Choose Tools SmartIcons.

   The SmartIcons dialog box appears.

2. From the list box at the top of the dialog box, choose the SmartIcon set you want to modify.

3. Drag the SmartIcon off the SmartIcon set.

To add a SmartIcon to the SmartIcon set

1. Choose Tools SmartIcons.

   The SmartIcons dialog box appears.

2. From the list box at the top of the dialog box, choose the SmartIcon set you want to modify.

3. Drag the SmartIcon from the Available Icons list box to any location on the SmartIcon set.

Note

See also *Macros*.

Sort

Purpose

Sorts lines, paragraphs, or table rows alphabetically or numerically, in ascending or descending order.

To sort the contents of a document

1. Select the text you want to sort.

   To sort the entire document, do not select any text.

   To sort table rows, place the insertion point within the table.

2. Choose Tools Sort.

   The Sort dialog box appears.

3. From the Sort Order options, choose the Ascending or Descending option button to specify the sorting order.

4. To customize how you want to sort data, choose the Field, Type, and Word options:

   From the Field column, specify the column by which you want to sort. Type a number in the Level text box, or click the up or down arrow to increase or decrease the number.

   From the Type column, choose Alphanumeric or Numeric.

   From the Word column, specify the number of words by which you want to sort. Choose 1st, 2nd, or All.

5. From the Delimiter options, specify the type of separator you want for columns in a multiple-column sort.

Choose the Tab Delimited or the Field Delimiter option.

Type a field delimiter character in the Field Delimiter text box.

6. Click OK or press Enter to begin sorting.

Note

The sort option information tells Ami Pro the type of sort and location of the field within the record. Ami Pro needs to know the location of the columns to sort them.

Spelling

Purpose

Checks the spelling in a document. You can use the Spelling feature to check a selected word or to find capitalization errors. You also can use the feature to find duplicate occurrences of a word, such as *the the*.

To check spelling

1. Place the insertion point where you want to begin checking spelling, or select the text you want to check.

2. Choose Tools Spell Check or click the Spell Check SmartIcon.

   The Spell Check dialog box appears.

3. To specify spelling checking the entire document, choose Beginning of Document and Include Other Text Streams.

4. Click OK or press Enter to start the spelling check.

Ami Pro displays the first unmatched word in the Replace With text box.

5. Choose one of the following options for the unmatched word:

Option	Effect
Skip	Does not change this occurrence of the word.
Skip All	Does not change any occurrence of the word.
Replace	Replaces the word with the word you type in the Replace With text box.
Replace All	Replaces all occurrences of the word with the word you type in the Replace With text box.
Add To Dictionary	Adds the word to the dictionary.
Cancel	Exits the Spelling feature.
Delete	Deletes the duplicate occurrence of the word.

After you choose an option, Ami Pro finds the next unmatched word.

Repeat this step.

If you make a mistake, you can undo the last correction with the Edit Undo command.

Starting Ami Pro

Purpose

Starts the Ami Pro program.

To start Ami Pro

1. At the C:> prompt, type WIN and press Enter to start Windows.

   The Windows Program Manager appears. The Ami Pro 3.0 group window contains the Ami Pro icon.

2. Double-click the Ami Pro icon.

   Ami Pro starts and displays a new, blank document window.

Styles

Purpose

Defines a group of paragraph and character formats as a *style* and saves the styles you define in a *style sheet*, a list of styles that are part of a document.

To create a style

If you want to base the new style on the style of particular text in the document, select that text before executing the following steps:

1. Choose Style Create Style.

   The Create Style dialog box appears.

2. Type a style name in the New Style text box.

3. Use one of the following Based On options:

   Choose the Style option, and then choose a style from the Style list box.

   Choose the Selected Text option.

4. Choose the Modify button.

   The Modify Style dialog box appears.

5. From the Modify area, choose a Modify option. Then specify any formats for the style.

6. Click OK or press Enter to add the style to the style sheet.

To modify a style

1. Choose Style Modify Style.

   The Modify Style dialog box appears.

2. Choose a style name in the Style text box.

3. From the Modify area, choose a Modify option. Then specify any formats for the style.

4. Click OK or press Enter to change the style in the style sheet.

To use a style

1. Use one of the following methods to indicate the style's range:

   To apply a style to one paragraph, place the insertion point anywhere in the paragraph.

   To apply a style to multiple paragraphs, select all or a portion of the paragraphs.

2. Choose the Styles box in the status bar, or choose Style Select a Style.

   The Style list box appears.

3. Choose the style you want to use.

Note

See also *Alignment, Fonts, Frames, Hyphenation, Page Breaks, Line Spacing,* and *Tables.*

Table of Authorities

Purpose

Generates a table of authorities for a legal brief.

You must run the TOA.SMM macro to create a table of authorities.

To run the table of authorities macro

1. Choose Tools Macros Playback.

2. In the Macros list box, choose the TOA.SMM macro.

3. Click OK or press Enter to run the macro.

   Ami Pro adds three commands to the Edit Mark Text menu—TOA Long Entry, TOA Short Entry, and Remove TOA Mark—and one command to the Tools menu—Generate TOA.

To mark table of authorities entries

1. Select the first citation you want to include in the table of authorities.

2. Choose Edit Mark Text.

3. Choose TOA Long Entry or TOA Short Entry.

   The TOA Long Entry or TOA Short Entry dialog box appears.

4. From the Category list box, choose the category you want to assign to the authority.

5. Click OK to mark the text.

6. Follow steps 1 through 5 to mark each authority you want to include in the table.

To remove a TOA mark

1. When you want to remove a TOA entry, choose Remove TOA Mark.

   The Remove TOA Entry dialog box appears.

2. From the existing entries list box, select the entries you want to remove.

3. Choose Long Citation on Page or Short Citation on Page. Specify the page number for the short citation by typing a page number in the text box or clicking the arrow next to the text box.

4. Choose the Remove button.

To generate a table of authorities

1. Mark the table of authorities entries in the document.

2. Place the insertion point at the beginning of the document.

3. Choose Tools Generate TOA.

   The Generate Table of Authorities dialog box appears.

4. In the Category Headings list box, choose the style you want to use for the category headings from the list of styles.

   Body Text is the default style.

5. In the References list box, choose the style you want to use for the references headings from the list of styles.

   Body Text is the default style.

6. In the Leader list box, choose a separator character.

7. Click OK or press Enter to generate the table of authorities.

Table of Contents

Purpose

Generates a table of contents for a document.

To mark table of contents entries

1. Select the first item you want to include in the table of contents.

2. Choose a heading style from the Styles box in the status bar.

3. Repeat steps 1 and 2 to apply heading styles to each item you want to include in the table of contents.

To generate a table of contents

1. Mark the table of contents entries in the document.

2. Place the insertion point at the beginning of the document.

3. Choose Tools TOC, Index.

   The TOC, Index dialog box appears.

4. Choose the TOC Options button.

   The TOC Options dialog box appears.

5. From the Style box list of styles, choose the style you want to use for entries at each level.

   Nine levels appear at the top of the TOC Options dialog box. The default styles appear in a list on the left side of the Style box, and the available styles appear in a list on the right side of the Style box. The available styles in the list display the level None.

   To specify a style and level in the Style box, first click the style. Then click the Promote button to move the style to a higher level or the Demote button to move the style to a lower level. Demote the styles you do not want to use in your table of contents to the None level.

6. In the Leader list box for each level, choose a separator character.

7. For each level, choose Page Number if you want to include page numbers in that TOC level.

8. To have page numbers appear aligned at the right margin, choose Right Align Page Number for each level for which you have chosen Page Number.

9. Click OK or press Enter to return to the TOC, Index dialog box.

10. In the Generate section, choose Table of Contents.

    If you want Ami Pro to place the table of contents in a separate file, type that file name in the TOC Output File text box. If you don't specify a file, Ami Pro places the table of contents at the beginning of the current document.

11. Click OK or press Enter to generate the table of contents.

Note

See also *Index*.

Tables

Purpose

Sets up tables so that you can organize items by columns and rows without calculating tab settings.

To create a table

1. Place the insertion point where you want the table to begin.

2. Choose Tools Tables.

   The Create Table dialog box appears.

3. Type the number of columns for the table in the Number of Columns text box and the number of rows for the table in the Number of Rows text box.

4. Choose the Layout button to specify table options.

5. To specify the width of the columns, type the column width in the Default Column Width text box, or click the up or down arrow to increase or decrease the width.

6. Click OK or press Enter to return to the Create Table dialog box.

7. Click OK or press Enter to accept your choices and return to the document.

   The table appears in the document.

8. Type the information into the table. Press Tab to move to the next cell in the row, or from the last cell in a row to the first cell in the next row.

To show or hide table lines

1. Select the table that contains the cells you want to modify.

2. Choose Table Lines & Color.

   The Lines & Color dialog box appears.

3. Mark or unmark the Line Position check boxes to add or remove lines. Line positions include All, Left, Right, Top, Bottom, and Outline.

4. Choose a line style from the Line Style list box.

5. To turn the cell color option on or off, mark or unmark the Fill Color check box. Choose a fill color from the color palette.

To insert a column or row

1. Use the appropriate insertion techniques from the following list:

   Place the insertion point in the column where you want the new column to appear.

   Place the insertion point in the row where you want the new row to appear.

2. Choose Table Insert Column/Row.

   Selected columns and all columns to the right move to the right after a column insertion. Selected rows and all rows below move down after a row insertion.

   The Insert Column/Row dialog box appears.

3. Choose the Columns option or Row option from the Insert Options area.

4. In the Number to Insert text box, specify the number of columns or rows to insert.

5. In the Position area, choose the Before or After option.

6. Click OK or press Enter.

    Existing columns move to the right, and existing rows move down.

To delete a column or row in a table

1. Select the columns or rows that you want to delete.

2. Choose Table Delete Column/Row.

    The Delete Column/Row dialog box appears.

3. Choose the Delete Column or Delete Row option.

4. Click OK or press Enter.

    Columns move to the left, and rows move up.

To connect cells

1. Select the cells that you want to connect to form a single cell.

2. Choose Table Connect Cells.

Note

A fast way to create a table is to click the Table SmartIcon on the SmartIcon set.

Tabs

Purpose

Sets left, center, numeric, right, and dot leader tabs.

To set or change tabs

1. Choose Page Modify Page Layout.

   The Modify Page Layout dialog box appears.

2. Use one of the following techniques:

   To set all new tabs, choose the Clear Tabs button.

   To change a specific tab, drag the tab marker off the Ruler.

3. From the Tab bar, choose the Left, Right, Numeric, or Center button.

   Choose the Leader button once for a solid line, twice for a dashed line, three times for a dotted line, and four times for no lines.

4. Type the new tab position in the Tabs text box and choose Set Tab.

5. Repeat steps 4 and 5 to set additional tabs.

6. Click OK or press Enter to confirm the tabs and return to the document.

Note

See also *Page Layout* and *Ruler*.

Text Attributes

Purpose

Enhances text and improves the look of documents.

You can use text attributes to emphasize important characters and words with bold, italic, or underline type. You also can change the appearance of individual letters, numbers, and symbols with caps and special effects.

To change text attributes

1. Select the text you want to change.

2. Choose Text.

3. Choose from the following Text Attribute options:

Option	Effect
Normal	Specifies using the existing style.
Bold	Specifies darkened text.
Italic	Specifies text in italics.
Underline	Specifies a single underline appearing under words and spaces (spaces made with the space bar, but not spaces made with tabs).
Word Underline	Specifies a single underline appearing only under words and not under spaces between words.

Option	Effect
Caps	Converts uppercase letters to lowercase and vice versa; converts words to initial cap and small caps. You can choose Upper Case, Lower Case, Initial Caps, or Small Caps.
Special Effects	Specifies the emphasis of the character. You can choose Superscript, Subscript, Double Underline, Strike-through, or Overstrike Character.

4. Click OK or press Enter to apply the text attributes.

Keyboard shortcuts

You also can use the following keyboard shortcuts to apply text attributes:

Format	Shortcut
Bold	Ctrl+B
Italic	Ctrl+I
Normal	Ctrl+N
Underline	Ctrl+U
Word underline	Ctrl+W

Notes

To restore a text attribute to the font setting of the paragraph, choose the Revert to Style check box in the Font dialog box.

To store a collection of font and text attributes and create a particular style to apply to a document, you can use the Style feature.

You can change text attributes by choosing Text, using the keyboard shortcuts, or clicking SmartIcons.

See also *Fonts*, *Page Layout*, *SmartIcons*, and *Styles*.

Thesaurus

Purpose

Looks up synonyms and antonyms without leaving the document.

To use the Thesaurus

1. Select the word for which you want to find synonyms or antonyms.

2. Choose Tools Thesaurus.

   The Thesaurus dialog box appears.

   Suggested synonyms appear in the Synonyms list box.

3. Choose from among the following options:

   To display synonyms that have different meanings, choose a different meaning from the Meaning Variations list box. Synonyms that have the chosen meaning now appear in the Synonyms list box.

To locate other meanings and synonyms, choose the Lookup button. Other meanings appear in the Meaning Variations list box, and other synonyms appear in the Synonyms list box.

To return to the previous word you looked up, choose the Previous button.

4. Choose one of the following alternatives:

To replace your word, choose the replacement word from the Synonyms list box. When the chosen word appears in the Replace With text box, choose the Replace button.

To close the dialog box without changing the word in the document, choose Cancel.

Tools User Setup

Purpose

Customizes Ami Pro options.

To choose the type of option to customize

1. Choose Tools User Setup.

   The User Setup dialog box appears.

2. Choose the setup options you want to customize:

Option	Effect
File Saving	Sets Auto backup and Auto timed save options.

Option	Effect
Undo Levels	Sets the number of times you can use undo to reverse the last action (maximum 4 levels).
Recent Files	Specifies the number of files that display at the bottom of the File menu.
Disable Warning Messages	Enables or disables warning messages.
Disable Online Help	Enables or disables on-line help.
Disable Drag Drop	Enables or disables & drag and drop features.
Notes	Sets name, initial, and color for notes in all documents.
Run Macros	Specifies the macros you can run when you load and exit Ami Pro.

Undo

Purpose

Reverses, undoes, or undeletes the most recent change to a document.

To use Undo

Choose Edit Undo or press Ctrl+Z.

Ami Pro reverses the most recent change to the document.

View

Purpose

Displays a document in full-page, custom, standard, enlarged, or facing-pages view. Also displays a document in layout mode, outline mode, or draft mode.

To view a document

1. Choose View.

2. Choose one of the following views:

Option	Effect
Full Page	Enables you to edit a document and display text and graphics (same as Print Preview in other DOS applications).
Custom	Enables you to type, edit, and format a document. You can set the percentage of magnification with the View View Preferences command.
Standard	Enables you to edit a document.
Enlarged	Enlarges the view of a page on-screen.
Facing Pages	Displays two facing pages side by side.

To change the view mode

1. Choose View.

2. Choose one of the following modes:

Option	Effect
Layout Mode	Displays how the document will look when printed (same as WYSIWYG).
Outline Mode	Enables you to create and view the outline structure of a document.
Draft Mode	Enables you to edit a document quickly. Displays less formatting.

INDEX